BRENDA GANTT

Live Each Little Moment Y'all

RECIPES & FELLOWSHIP FROM MY KITCHEN

83
PRESS

83 PRESS®

Copyright ©2024 by 83 Press

83 Press
2323 2nd Avenue North
Birmingham, AL 35203
83press.com

ISBN 979-8-9899185-2-2
Printed in USA.

BRENDA GANTT

Live Each Little Moment Y'all

RECIPES & FELLOWSHIP FROM MY KITCHEN

INTRODUCTION

Dear friends and family,

What a year we have had together! The busyness of life has made us all realize the value of each little moment. The fact that each moment will never be exactly the same ever again should cause us to look at life's moments very differently.

A good example is how a little boy reacts when he sees a big mud puddle after a heavy rain. He doesn't ask if he can jump in. He doesn't even think about getting permission. He just jumps right into the puddle and starts playing. As the boy's mother gazes at him splashing in the puddle, she has choices. Her thoughts and attitude can be: 1. I'm going out there and fuss at him for this. 2. Oh my, I'll never get those clothes clean again. 3. How could my child do such a thing? I've taught him better than this. 4. There are so many germs in that puddle; I'm positive he'll get sick. 5. What will my neighbors think if they see this? Or, the boy's mother can look at this as a special time that will never be quite the same ever again. She can jump in the puddle with him or have a mud fight or make a mud pie. It's all in how we look at the moments that happen in our daily life. Live each little moment, y'all! Remember, that exact moment will never happen again. Make the best of it! You can turn moments into bad or good ones, depending on your attitude.

All my cookbooks have special titles. They are not just words; they are my heartfelt longings. Let's strive to live each little moment and be thankful we are still able to jump in the mud puddles!

Live!

Brenda Hantt

CONTENTS

DEDICATION

My George, my soulmate, my sweetheart,

I lovingly and proudly dedicate this cookbook to you. I miss your touch, your voice, your laughter, and your strong hand holding me tight. Every time I make a new recipe, I think of what you always said: "Hope you wrote this recipe down, baby. It's delicious."

As I write this dedication, tears well up in my eyes. I think back on our time together and all the little moments we shared like drinking hot coffee together on the porch swing on chilly mornings or planning our building projects while on long trips in our truck. I'll always remember how you loved and hugged our children. Recalling your manly strut always makes me smile. I think of you, standing in the woods in old, dirty work clothes with a power saw in one hand and a canning jar full of iced tea in the other. All the memories hang here in my heart, and I just pull them out when I'm alone and missing you.

Thank you for leading our entire family in the path of Jesus. Your grandchildren adored you, and you would be proud of them. Bay and Isabella are in college now becoming adults. Cape starts college this fall. She will have some adjustments to make—of that, I'm sure. Banks has turned into a beautiful teenager, as bossy as ever. Your William is now 16 and loves driving his truck just like you did. He still fishes and talks about his memories of fishing with you. Our Hannah misses you so. She reminisces about how you always hugged her tight when she would enter through the den door. I think your hugs were her security. She still loves dirt and gardening just like you did.

You would be proud of your Dallas. He follows in your footsteps, always counseling others and leading them in the way of Christ. He's teaching his children

just as you taught him. He thinks of you and often says, "I wonder what Daddy is doing right now as he walks around Heaven." Anna is busy moving into their new home. She's using lots of the beautiful antiques you taught her to love. She's still making tasty desserts for the family. Walt works at his building projects and remembers everything you taught him about living the Christian life and being a loving daddy and husband. You taught him so much.

We are all living and doing the best we can. We worship; we go on vacation; we work hard, and we remember you and your ways. We know this life is short at best. Heaven awaits, and one day, we will all be together again. Until then, we will cherish each little moment we had together. We will love, laugh, cry, worship, sing, work hard, pray, and eat lots of good food. And me, well, I will let the children take care of me until I come to you. I love you, sweetheart.

Always and forever,
Brenda

"The motion of an old, wooden swing
has birthed many songs, poems,
prayers, tears, and ideas from the ones
who have rested there."

GOOD SALT

FOREWORD BY WALT MERRELL

The art of cooking has a finicky appetite. Chefs, some might say, are masters of their domain. Chefs prepare food and do it with brilliant skill. A cook, though, a really good cook, soothes people with the food they bring to the table. You might even say a good cook has mastered the art of bringing people joy.

Brenda Gantt, or Big Mama, as we call her, brings people joy even before she cracks the first egg or kneads the first handful of dough. She brings people joy because she is more than a chef; she is a good cook. And I'm not really speaking to her abilities in the kitchen but rather the woman that she is. Maybe, it is her infectious smile or her sweet spirit, but whatever it is, she brings people joy. Jesus reminded His followers that they "are the salt of the earth." Big Mama is salt. In fact, she is "good salt." And what self-respecting Southerner doesn't like some good salt in the recipe of their life?

People often ask me if Brenda acts and talks and lives the same way in real life as she does when the camera is on. I easily and quickly answer "yes," because she is not only good salt but real salt, too. The Southern twang, great big smile, and ever cheerful personality—that's all real, and that's all my mother-in-law. What you see is exactly what you get, and we need more of it in this world today.

Big Mama is as down-home as an old dirt road. She is as reliable as a 200-year-old oak tree. She is as loving as a mother doe to her newborn fawn, and she is as honest

as the day is long. She is a true Proverbs 31 woman who is selfless to her own detriment. I have lost count of how many times she stopped what she was doing to tend to one of our girls. But that's who she is. She loves, and that is why I love her. She doesn't seek fame or fortune. In fact, she shies away from the attention.

Refusing offers for television shows and fancy new appliances in her kitchen, Big Mama prefers the quiet comfort of home and her simple role as a teacher with a rather large classroom! She loves helping others. And what better way to help someone—especially young married couples—than by teaching them the joy that comes from being in the kitchen together and sitting around the table longer than you probably should. Big Mama is a great cook because she understands the joy that comes from preparing food has more to do with what happens at the table than it does with what is on the plate.

Not that the good, tasty food isn't important. It is. And, she really is a great chef, too, but she understands the importance of spending time together and how the meal she cooks can bring her entire family to the same place in a little moment of togetherness. She is a true matriarch, but her ambition is only to love her family, and that includes you. That, my friends, is good salt. Salt is that extra something special that makes the difference. That's Big Mama in a nutshell. She is something special to all of us, and she makes a difference in every one of our lives, too.

GRANDBABIES

Grandbabies are God's greatest gift to old folks like me. I may ache; I may be sad; I may be lonesome; or I may be tired, but as soon as I look upon their smiling faces or feel their tight hugs, it all seems to disappear. My love and concern for them is told to the Lord in my daily prayers. I wish I could fix any problems they might have. I can't, but God can.

Banks finally made it to Andalusia High School. She will be a cheerleader and a member of the color guard under the Friday night lights. Even though she's older now, she still loves cooking in the kitchen. But spending the night with me is getting less frequent—friends spend-the-night parties have taken priority.

Bay is a senior at the University of Mississippi, or "Ole Miss," and is a member of the Chi Omega sorority. She's majoring in Southern Studies with a minor in Museum Studies. Bay loves dumplings and BLT sandwiches. Hugging is a great quality that sets her apart from others. She gives the best hugs ever.

Cape is a freshman at Mississippi State University. She's majoring in Aerospace Engineering with a minor in Leadership Studies. Her favorite foods are creamed corn, seafood, and French onion soup. Cape is known for speaking her mind. I don't always agree with her, but she's honest with her thoughts.

William is a junior at American Christian Academy this year. His favorite thing to do on weekends is jump in his truck, grab his fishing pole, and head to any body of water he can find. William loves chicken salad, fried catfish, and collards. He helps me any time I ask him without complaining.

Isabella is a sophomore at the University of Alabama and is a member of the Phi Mu sorority. She is majoring in Architectural Engineering with a minor in Business. Isabella loves crab cakes, casseroles, and all veggies. I always enjoy hearing her laugh; it gets everybody laughing with her.

Whenever Discouraged...

You are only one.
But, you are one.
You cannot do Everything.
But, you can do Something.
And what you can do.
You ought to do.
And By the Grace of God
You will do.

From Brenda Gantt
Recipe Box
1968

"Just for You"
Throughout the chapters of
This cookbook You'll find some
of our life's little moments.
Each story tells of a simple, but
special memory. Time spent
together is priceless for sure!
      You'll also see some of our
favorite collections. George
and I enjoyed the adventures
of looking...trash piles, antique
shops, junk shops, and
estate sales for our treasures
Ya'll know that the fun is
in the HUNT!! So, get
out there and find the
treasures you like!
                    Brenda Gantt
                              2024

chapter 1

SUNNY-SIDE UP

EYES OF A CHILD

The local JCPenney store employees knew my son's name by heart. Why? Because they heard me calling his name every single time I went shopping there. At 3½ years old, Dallas could disappear from my side in a heartbeat. I'd be calling his name while holding my baby, Hannah, in my arms. (Remember, back then, we didn't have backpacks or car seats to hold our babies.) You can picture me as a young mama with a panicked voice that could be heard from one end of the store to the other. When the other customers heard me, they would also start to call out his name. Heck, back then, everybody tried to help look after other folks' little ones.

Y'all remember those round clothing racks that are in the middle of the department store? Dallas would climb on a bar near the bottom of those racks and hide between the dresses. We'd hear him laughing and giggling as he hid among all the tightly packed clothing. Occasionally, he'd poke his cute, little face out and smile. He was having a great time playing hide-and-seek even though I was still in panic mode. Once I finally found him, it was hard to decide whether to fuss at him or to hug him tight. On one shopping trip, we found him in the showcase window with all the mannequins. He was holding their hands and looking out of the window at all the people walking by. I can only imagine what they were thinking. I guess he just had a playful heart—and I'm thankful for it. He never lost that playful heart. Even today as a full-grown man with children of his own, he loves to joke around with his kids, William and Isabella. It just tickles him to death when they get aggravated at his humor.

Sometimes, I think we should look at life through the eyes of a child. Then, we would love more, laugh more, forgive more quickly, play more, dance in the rain, and look at the world with a special wonder in our eyes and hearts.

FRENCH TOAST BAKE

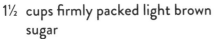

The flavor of French toast is so good—everybody loves it! This casserole gives you a fresh way to enjoy this sweet, delicious breakfast food.

1½ cups firmly packed light brown sugar
1 stick salted butter
¼ cup plus 2 tablespoons corn syrup
10 to 12 slices French bread
4 large eggs
1½ cups whole milk
1 tablespoon vanilla extract
¼ teaspoon salt
3 tablespoons granulated sugar
1½ teaspoons ground cinnamon
½ stick salted butter (melted)

1. Grease a 13x9-inch casserole dish. In a saucepan, cook brown sugar, butter, and corn syrup over medium heat, stirring constantly, until bubbling, about 5 minutes. Pour the syrup mixture into the prepared dish. Arrange bread slices on top.
2. Combine the eggs, milk, vanilla, and salt. Pour over the top of bread. Refrigerate overnight.
3. Preheat oven to 350°.
4. Combine granulated sugar, cinnamon, and melted butter and drizzle over the top of casserole.
5. Bake, uncovered, until bubbly and set, about 45 to 50 minutes.

Spring in south Alabama brings baby tadpoles in every mud puddle near and far. As children, Dallas and Hannah loved to bring an empty fruit jar along on our walks down dirt roads through our woods. They'd capture a jarful of tadpoles, bring them back home, and watch them turn into frogs. Yes, our home turned into a frog nursery, but these little moments were priceless.

BACON CHEESE BISCUITS

Now that you have all learned from my first book how to make those Buttermilk Biscuits with White Lily flour, do some experimenting. You will love this recipe for a starter. Be brave and think of some different ways to spice up or sweeten up your homemade biscuits.

Shortening to grease
2½ cups White Lily self-rising flour
1   stick salted butter (frozen)
1   cup whole buttermilk
5   pieces thick-cut bacon (fried and chopped)
1   cup grated sharp Cheddar cheese
2   tablespoons butter (melted)

1. Preheat oven to 500°. Grease a large cast-iron skillet with shortening.
2. Sift flour in a medium-size bowl. Grate frozen butter in with the flour and use your hands to mix. Add the buttermilk, bacon, and cheese; mix well.
3. Lightly flour the counter. Put the dough on the counter and fold it over several times. Cut the biscuits out. Makes approximately 18 biscuits.
4. Bake on the middle rack of the oven until golden brown, 10 to 12 minutes.
5. Brush melted butter on top of biscuits.

AND HE SAID UNTO THEM, TAKE HEED, AND BEWARE OF COVETOUSNESS: FOR A MAN'S LIFE CONSISTETH NOT IN THE ABUNDANCE OF THE THINGS WHICH HE POSSESSETH. —LUKE 12:15, KJV

CHOCOLATE GRAVY

I didn't grow up having chocolate gravy. In fact, I had never heard of it until one of my social media followers, a guest at The Cottle House Bed & Breakfast, told me all about it. She actually wrote down the recipe for me. Her mama made it on special occasions like a birthday, Christmas, or Thanksgiving. I made my own version.

1   stick salted butter
1   cup sugar
3   tablespoons unsweetened cocoa powder
¼   cup White Lily self-rising flour
3   cups whole milk
½   cup water

1. Melt butter in a cast-iron skillet over medium heat. (I like a thick, black skillet as it keeps butter from scorching.)
2. In a bowl, mix sugar, cocoa, and flour and stir well. Gradually add milk, 1 to 2 tablespoons at a time, to sugar mixture, stirring after each addition, until you have a pudding texture. Then, add remaining milk and ½ cup water, stirring well.
3. Combine this chocolate mixture with the melted butter in the skillet. Whisk well. Cook over medium-low heat until gravy is hot and thick. If the gravy seems too thick to pour on a biscuit, add a tad of water until you get the correct thickness.

Walt waiting for a picnic feast

Banks has spent many hours in my kitchen, and I'm so thankful she did. Here, she's making biscuits for breakfast. I have loved every little moment with her, even if flour ended up everywhere.

KITCHEN WISDOM

If you have leftover gravy, you can save it in the refrigerator, but note that the gravy solidifies when cold. To serve, you'll need to add a little water or milk, mix it up with a whisk, and slowly heat it back up over medium-low heat.

HOMEMADE HASH BROWNS

This is a wonderful breakfast dish to serve with fried eggs, bacon, and biscuits—or serve it at night with pork chops. This recipe makes one large patty that can be shared.

1   large russet or Idaho potato (unpeeled)
4   tablespoons olive oil
Salt and black pepper to taste

1. Using the largest holes of a box grater, grate the entire potato.
2. Heat oil in a skillet or on a griddle over medium heat. Put grated potato in center of pan, making a flat and round shape like a pancake. Mash flat with a spatula.
3. Season with salt and pepper. Cook until brown and crispy on bottom side. Use a spatula to turn the potato cake over to the other side to brown, being careful not to break it apart. Add a tad more oil, if you need.

"Solid wood furniture will last for generations. Cheap furniture will wind up in the burn pile."

Life's Collections

By now everyone knows I love old things. Well, the birdhouses I collect are made of old wood from barns, houses, furniture, porch rails, and beadboards. The paint is warm, and the roofs are tin, slate, or faded boards. Most of mine are in the shape of churches with beautiful steeples.

REDEYE GRAVY

—◆—

Split open a biscuit and put a little Redeye Gravy on each side.
This recipe only makes a small amount of gravy, so you will have to put butter
and jelly on your other biscuit. It's great on grits, too!

1   teaspoon bacon grease
1   package country ham (cut into
    5 to 7 pieces)
⅓   cup water

1. Smear bacon grease in a 9-inch cast-iron skillet. (Be sure to put 1 teaspoon only.) Add the ham and cook over medium heat on one side until browned. Turn it and repeat on the other side. Remove browned ham from skillet. Pour all the grease into a small bowl.

2. Heat the empty skillet over medium heat. Pour ⅓ cup water into the hot empty skillet. (This pulls up all the goodie on the bottom of the skillet.) Cook 2 seconds. Pour water slowly into the small bowl of grease. Stir.

Grandbabies have fun at the farm in Pickens County, Alabama.

Sisters sunning on the beach in Pensacola, Florida, from left to right, Lucille, Kitty, my Grannie Hicks (Bertha Viola Jones), and Hattie B

KITCHEN WISDOM

Some people put leftover coffee in the skillet instead of the water. I personally like water in mine because I want to taste the ham flavor. The coffee seems to overpower the taste of the country ham.

PECAN UPSIDE-DOWN CAKE

A real crowd-pleaser, this cake is so nice and moist. Serve it for breakfast, brunch, or dinner. I enjoy it straight out of the oven while it's still warm.

1 (15.25-ounce) box yellow cake mix
1 (3.4-ounce) package vanilla instant pudding
3 large eggs (beaten)
½ cup vegetable oil
1 cup water
1 stick salted butter (melted)
¾ cup light brown sugar
1 cup pecans (chopped)

1. Preheat oven to 350°. Grease and flour a 15-cup Bundt pan.
2. Beat together cake mix, pudding, eggs, oil, and 1 cup water. Set aside.
3. Pour melted butter into bottom of prepared pan. Sprinkle butter with brown sugar. Layer pecans over the brown sugar mixture. Pour prepared batter over pecans.
4. Bake until a wooden pick comes out clean, 35 to 45 minutes. Let cool in the pan for 5 minutes and then invert onto a serving plate. Be sure to scrape the goodie out of the bottom of the pan and sprinkle on top.

I love gardening, and I use flowers from my yard to make pretty arrangements for my home.

GOOD MORNING CAKE

Sometimes, you want something different to start your day. This cake will hit the spot! We cut nice, big slices and enjoy it with some hot coffee. When the weather is good, we like to eat our breakfast on the porch and sip coffee as long as time allows.

1   cup granulated sugar
1   cup light brown sugar
1   cup White Lily self-rising flour
1   cup chopped pecans
½   cup vegetable oil
4   large eggs
2   tablespoons ground cinnamon
1   teaspoon ground cloves
Powdered sugar

1. Preheat oven to 350°.
2. Mix together granulated sugar, brown sugar, flour, pecans, oil, eggs, cinnamon, and cloves. Pour batter into a greased 10-inch cast-iron skillet or 13x9-inch baking dish.
3. Bake for 30 minutes. Loosely cover with foil to prevent overbrowning and bake until a wooden pick comes out clean, 15 minutes more. Dust with powdered sugar.

Bay and Cape pose in Big Mama's kitchen, sharing one pair of house shoes, you might notice. I always loved for them to spend the night.

Isabella tastes the icing to make sure it is good.

GRITS CASSEROLE

We are always so busy on the mornings of Christmas, Thanksgiving, and Easter. This hearty casserole will ease your burden and stress during the holidays or when you have overnight visitors. Make this dish the day before, pop it in the oven in the morning, and voilà, your problem is solved. My grandchildren William and Isabella love to have grits when they come to visit me.

4½ cups water
1½ cups old-fashioned grits
1 stick salted butter
1 pound ground sausage
3 large eggs (slightly beaten)
1½ cups whole milk
2½ cups grated sharp Cheddar cheese
Fried eggs

1. Preheat oven to 350°. Grease a 13x9-inch casserole dish with butter.

Isabella, William, and Cape show their school spirit.

2. Pour 4½ cups water into a heavy-bottomed stockpot. Whisk in grits and add butter. Bring to a boil over medium-high heat. Now, put the whisk away and get out a strong, stiff spatula. Lower the heat to medium and cook, using the spatula to stir the grits, for 20 minutes. (Don't let the grits stick to the bottom!)
3. In a skillet, cook the sausage until browned and crumbled. Drain and divide into 2 small bowls.
4. Combine the beaten eggs with milk and stir well. Set aside.
5. Put half of the sausage in the bottom of the casserole dish (save the other half for the top).
6. Take the grits off the heat. Let cool for 5 minutes and then mix in the egg mixture with the grits. Stir in 2 cups cheese.
7. Pour the grits mixture over the sausage in the dish. Then, sprinkle the remaining sausage and remaining ½ cup cheese on top of the casserole. Cover with foil.
8. Bake until set, 45 to 50 minutes. Serve with fried eggs.

KITCHEN WISDOM

If you make this dish ahead to cook for the next day, take it out of the refrigerator at least 1 hour before you put it in the oven.

SAUSAGE BALLS

Hannah shared this recipe with me, and I just love to make it. While these are great for breakfast, they also make a tasty afternoon snack for a hungry teenager.

1   (16-ounce) package ground pork sausage
1   cup White Lily all-purpose flour
1   cup grated sharp Cheddar cheese
1   (4-ounce) package cream cheese (room temperature)
1   (1-ounce) envelope ranch seasoning mix
3   green onions (chopped)

1. Preheat oven to 350°.
2. In a large bowl, combine all ingredients, kneading by hand until mixture forms one big ball. Make sure all the flour and cheese are combined well with the sausage.
3. Begin rolling the sausage mixture into walnut-size balls. Place on an ungreased baking sheet.
4. Bake until golden brown, about 25 minutes. Serve warm.

EAT MY WORDS

Before George and I had children, we were watching TV one night and saw a well-dressed lady in New York City with a harness and leash around her child as they walked through the crowded streets. As soon as I saw it, I said to George, "That's awful! I will never do that when we have children." Glory! Did I ever eat my words! If there's one thing in life that's true, it's that we all must take back our words from time to time. I didn't put a harness and leash on Dallas, but I can surely say that he probably needed one. The lesson is: never say what you will or will not do, and never say what your children will or will not do. One day, you will have to get out the salt and pepper because you will surely be eating your words.

⁓⁓⁓

chapter 2

THIS AND THATS

HUCKLEBERRIES & LITTLE NOSES

In the great year of 1975, George and I moved our little family into our newly built home right in the middle of Sweet Gum Bottom Woods. Dallas and

Hannah were just babies. We were in our 20s and didn't know much about raising children or building houses. We were learning as we went on our way.

George's parents owned many acres of beautiful, wooded land and gave us 5 acres of our choice to build our home. Wanting to please me, George told me to pick out any spot that I wanted. I couldn't resist one particular area with its tall virgin pines and an understory of blossoming white native dogwood trees everywhere. It was absolutely gorgeous!

The woods were thick with huckleberry bushes, vines, yaupons, and hollies that grew within 15 feet from our home. As George's Uncle Pickens would always say, "These woods are so thick that you can't poke your lips out to whistle."

One morning, we were so busy planting azalea bushes in the small front yard that we didn't even notice that Dallas and Hannah were picking huckleberries and sticking them up their noses. I'm not talking about one or two—I'm talking a snoot-full of berries. Dallas was about 3½ years old, and Hannah was two years younger than him, so we panicked when we saw what they had done.

George grabbed them up, and we flew inside the house straight to the kitchen sink. We told Dallas to blow his nose really hard so that most of the berries would come out. But Hannah was too little and had not yet learned to blow her nose. We laid her on the kitchen counter, got some eyebrow tweezers, and pulled out those huckleberries, one by one, while Hannah screamed to high heaven. We used a flashlight to see if we got them all. We could see that one, maybe two, were still in her tiny nose. About ready to go to the emergency room, we tried one more time. With Hannah screaming louder than ever, we successfully plucked out every last huckleberry. Y'all know mamas and daddies are sometimes surgeons along with their other professions! It's a miracle that any parent can successfully raise a child to adulthood. We do our best and pray to the good Lord to cover all the rest of our blunders.

SHRIMP DIP

This is a great, quick dip. Just keep a can or two of shrimp in your pantry and then you'll always have it handy to make a fancy dish when friends drop by unexpectedly.

1 (8-ounce) package cream cheese (softened)
1 (8-ounce) container sour cream
2 (6-ounce) cans medium shrimp (drained)
¼ cup green onion (chopped small)
¼ cup chopped celery
1 tablespoon fresh lemon juice
½ teaspoon ground red pepper (more if you like it spicy)
Fancy crackers

1. Using a stand mixer, beat cream cheese and sour cream. Stir in shrimp, green onion, celery, lemon juice, and red pepper. Chill. Serve with crackers.

Bay at her graduation from Little Friends Preschool

Life's Little Moments

In the spring, blackberries and dewberries grow wild in the South. We'd take empty ice-cream buckets, and all head out to find them, always eating more of them than we put in the buckets! With our arms and hands scratched up from the thorns of the berry bushes, we would finally gather enough to take home. Dividing the berries into soup bowls, we sprinkled lots of sugar on top, poured cold milk into the bowls, and stirred as we watched the milk turn purple in color—then we gobbled them up.

ALFREDO SAUCE

You can do so much with this sauce! You don't have to use broccoli. Try it with chicken, crabmeat, or asparagus, or eat it just plain over pasta.

1 small onion (diced)
½ stick salted butter
3 teaspoons olive oil
3 cloves garlic (minced)
2 cups whole milk
1 cup chicken broth
1 teaspoon dried Italian seasoning
½ teaspoon salt
¼ teaspoon black pepper
4 tablespoons White Lily all-purpose flour
4 tablespoons water
1 cup heavy whipping cream
1 (5-ounce) package grated Parmesan cheese
1 (12.6-ounce) package broccoli florets (steamed)
1 (16-ounce) package linguine or spaghetti (cooked according to package directions)

1. In a pot, sauté onion in butter and olive oil until tender. Add garlic and cook for 1 minute, stirring continuously. Add milk, broth, Italian seasoning, salt, and pepper. Bring milk mixture to a low boil. Stir continuously.

2. In a small bowl or cup, mix flour and 4 tablespoons water, stirring with a fork until there are no lumps.

3. Add cream to milk mixture and stir. Add flour mixture and cook until sauce thickens, stirring for a few minutes with a spatula so mixture doesn't stick to the bottom of the pot. Add cheese, stirring until melted.

4. Put cooked pasta on a plate, top with steamed broccoli, and pour sauce on top. Serve with garlic bread and salad.

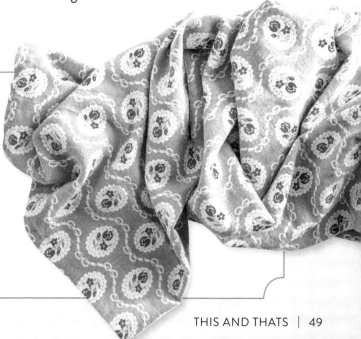

SUBMIT YOURSELVES THEREFORE TO GOD. RESIST THE DEVIL, AND HE WILL FLEE FROM YOU. DRAW NIGH TO GOD, AND HE WILL DRAW NIGH TO YOU. CLEANSE YOUR HANDS, YE SINNERS; AND PURIFY YOUR HEARTS, YE DOUBLE MINDED. —JAMES 4:7–8, KJV

SLUMGULLY

I don't know who invented the name for this recipe, but it's basically just okra and tomatoes. "Slumgully" is what we always called it.

1   (16-ounce) package frozen cut okra (not breaded)
2   (14.5-ounce) cans petite diced tomatoes (undrained)
Salt and black pepper to taste

1. In a stainless steel skillet, cook okra and tomatoes over medium heat until some of the juice from the tomatoes has partially cooked out. Make sure the okra pieces are tender.

2. Season with salt and pepper. Serve it along with other foods or eat it over rice. This is even better if the vegetables are straight out of the garden.

Many of you have asked about my chopping block. I have had it a long time. George and I found it in Selma, Alabama, and it had no legs. It's a solid block of wood, and George added the legs. This is Bay as a baby sitting under it about 21 years ago.

Life's Collections

Hannah gave me this pig bowl one Christmas. She said she thought of me when she saw it. It works perfectly for all my rocks. Friends and family have given me rocks from their travels. Some unusual ones I found at home or on trips.

SAUSAGE DOGS

Whether you're heading to the ballpark to watch a Little League game or staying home to watch a big ball game on TV, sauerkraut and sausage on a bun is the perfect combination.

2 pounds smoked sausage (cut to fit on buns)
½ cup water
Sauerkraut
1 package buns
Brenda's Spicy Mustard (recipe at right)

1. Preheat oven to 400°.
2. In a cast-iron skillet, combine the sausage and ½ cup water. Cover with foil.
3. Bake for 35 to 40 minutes, depending on the thickness of the sausage. Remove the foil and bake until sausage is browned.
4. In a skillet, heat the sauerkraut over medium heat.
5. Place the buns on a pan and cover with foil. Bake until heated, just 1 to 2 minutes.
6. Put 1 sausage piece on each bun and build it with Brenda's Spicy Mustard and warm sauerkraut. Add any other toppings you desire.

BRENDA'S SPICY MUSTARD

Use this mustard on hot dogs, sausage, sandwiches, or anything that you want to have a little spiciness.

1 cup prepared yellow mustard
½ cup light brown sugar
½ teaspoon ground turmeric
¼ teaspoon ground ginger
¼ teaspoon ground cinnamon
⅛ teaspoon ground nutmeg

1. Mix together all ingredients and enjoy. Easy peasy!

"Being on time is like honey to the one waiting."

KITCHEN WISDOM

People like all manner of toppings on their Sausage Dogs. You can use pickles, onions, green onions, ketchup, and mayonnaise, if you like it. But it's best topped with Brenda's Spicy Mustard.

SALMON SALAD

Salmon is so good for you! You can serve this like a dip with bread, crackers, or even vegetables. If you're really hungry, it makes a great sandwich, too.

1 (14.75-ounce) can pink salmon (drained)
2 tablespoons sweet pickle relish
1 stalk celery (diced)
½ small onion (diced)
Mayonnaise (enough to make salad creamy)
Toasted crackers or bread

1. Mix all ingredients together, and it's ready!
2. Serve with crackers or toasted bread.

Livingston State College Flag Girls. I'm in the front row on the right reaching my hand toward the center. I wish I still had my white boots with the tassles. Mama must have given them away.

I am snuggling before bedtime with Isabella.

KITCHEN WISDOM

If you ever have leftover cooked salmon, you could use two forks to break it up and use it instead of canned. Most people think the only fish to make a salad out of is tuna. Try salmon.

BRENDA'S SPINACH AND PORK CHOP POTATOES

Making up recipes is always a fun thing to do. Sometimes, George and I would be so hungry that I would just make up a new recipe on the spot. It would turn out delicious, and George would say, "I hope you wrote this recipe down." Then, I'd say, "Sorry, I have no clue what I put in it." This Spinach and Pork Chop Potatoes recipe is one that I actually wrote down—thank goodness I did!

2 to 3 pork chops (cut into cubes)
1   teaspoon onion salt
1   teaspoon garlic powder
2   tablespoons Worcestershire sauce
4 to 5 Idaho potatoes (peeled and cubed)
2   tablespoons olive oil
1   medium yellow onion (cubed)
1   medium green bell pepper (diced)
6   green onions (chopped, green and white parts)
1   bag fresh spinach leaves (not chopped)
Sour cream

1. Place pork chop pieces in a bowl. Sprinkle with onion salt, garlic powder, and Worcestershire sauce. Stir well, making sure to coat each piece of meat. Set aside to marinate.
2. Place potatoes in large pot and cover with water. Bring to a boil over medium heat and cook until fork tender. Drain in a colander.
3. In a large skillet, sauté pork in olive oil over medium heat. Add onion and bell pepper, and cook until onion is tender. Add green onions and spinach leaves. When spinach leaves are nice and wilted, turn heat off.
4. Place potatoes in individual serving bowls and top with pork chop mixture. Add a dollop of sour cream on top.

I love to make up recipes, and George always let me know when one was really good.

"Don't settle for cheaply made things. It's like throwing your money in the wind."

BAKED HOT WINGS

———

Hey, y'all can cook these wings at home! Don't think you have to go out to eat and pay a small fortune for hot wings. It's messy, so grab a cloth napkin in hand and sit down. Enjoy home-cooked wings. What a treat!

1   cup water
1   cup White Lily all-purpose flour
1   tablespoon paprika
1   teaspoon garlic powder
1   teaspoon light brown sugar
1   teaspoon salt
1   teaspoon black pepper
12 to 16 chicken wings (you can cut
      them in half if you prefer)
Celery stalks
Homemade Dill Ranch (recipe at right)
Hot wing sauce of your choice

1. Preheat oven to 400°.
2. Grease the top of a broiler pan. Put 1 cup water in the bottom of the pan.
3. Mix flour, paprika, garlic powder, brown sugar, salt, and pepper in a large bowl. Add chicken wings to the flour mixture and toss until each wing is well coated. Place the wings on the prepared pan.
4. Bake for 20 minutes. Turn the wings to the other side and bake until browned, 20 minutes more.
5. Serve with celery, Homemade Dill Ranch, and a bottle of your favorite hot wing sauce.

HOMEMADE DILL RANCH

———

So many people love ranch dressing, including the folks in my family. I added a little dill to this homemade version to give it a fresh taste.

1   cup mayonnaise
½   cup sour cream
½   cup whole buttermilk
1   teaspoon fresh lemon juice
¾   teaspoon dried dill
¾   teaspoon dried chives
½   teaspoon dried parsley
½   teaspoon garlic powder
¼   teaspoon onion powder
¼   teaspoon salt
½   teaspoon black pepper

1. In a small bowl, mix mayonnaise, sour cream, and buttermilk until smooth. Stir in lemon juice, dill, chives, parsley, garlic powder, onion powder, salt, and pepper.

CHEESY TOMATOES

*Beautiful summer tomatoes sat on a platter in my kitchen window.
They were big and juicy, so I decided to make up a recipe to use them. That was
several years ago, and this dish is still one of my favorite snacks on a warm
summer day. Porch life at its best!*

2 large summer tomatoes (cut into
  nice, thick slices)
Grated cheeses (sharp Cheddar,
  mozzarella, Gouda, pepper Jack, or
  any combination of cheeses you like)
Herbs and spices (garlic powder, dried
  Italian seasoning, oregano, rosemary,
  or any others you like)

1. Preheat oven to 400°.
2. Separate tomato slices and place on
a lightly greased baking dish or sheet.
Sprinkle cheese on each slice. Sprinkle
spices all over the cheese.
3. Bake until cheese is bubbling and
slightly brown around the edges. Enjoy
while the tomatoes are still warm.

Kids will be kids. Even the old ones love to put their toes in the pond.

Brenda Ann Hicks Gantt. This little dress was pink and purple. I loved it.

SPINACH DIP

—————◆—————

Y'all, I know you have probably made this dip for years, but I wanted to have it in my book because we don't want the recipe to be lost. My whole family can devour an entire bowl in a matter of an hour. I want my grandchildren to always know that their Big Mama loved Spinach Dip. Everybody loves it!

2 (12-ounce) packages frozen chopped spinach
1 (8-ounce) can sliced water chestnuts (drained and chopped)
1 cup mayonnaise
1 cup sour cream
1 (1.4-ounce) envelope dry vegetable soup mix
4 green onions (chopped)
Fancy crackers

1. Let spinach thaw and drain. Using your hands, squeeze the extra liquid out.
2. In a bowl, mix together spinach, water chestnuts, mayonnaise, sour cream, soup mix, and green onions. Serve with crackers.

George and I celebrated our 70th birthdays with our grandbabies.

"When you take this Spinach Dip to a party, you will always come home with an empty bowl."

————— KITCHEN WISDOM —————

Remember to actually put the spinach in your hands and squeeze out every drop of liquid, or your dip will be runny.

PECAN KISSES

—◆—

*I pull out a wicker basket with a pretty tea towel and fill it with these treats.
With just the right amount of sugar, the wonderful pecan flavor shines through.
You won't be able to eat just a few—you'll grab a handful.*

1 large egg white
½ teaspoon vanilla extract
¾ cup light brown sugar
2 cups pecan halves

1. Preheat oven to 250°.
2. Beat egg white until it forms soft peaks. Gradually stir in vanilla and brown sugar. Add pecans and stir gently until all are well coated.
3. Drop mixture by tablespoonfuls on a lightly greased or parchment-lined baking sheet. Make sure to keep at least 1 inch apart.
4. Bake for 30 minutes. Let cool on the pan.

Collections are found in every room of my home. Don't you wish everything still came in glass bottles instead of plastic? Do y'all remember glass milk jugs?

Bay, Banks, and Cape

chapter 3

SERVING & SHARING

THE UNEXPECTED

Banks is always popping in at the most unexpected times. If I'm in the back room doing crafts, writing, or painting, she will bang on the window to get my attention. I always get up from my chair to let in that happy little face.

One particular day, I had made a big, beautiful cake and had it sitting on a pedestal cake plate covered with a clear, etched dome. It looked like a Queen sitting on her throne. As Banks came through the door, she spied the cake, got my old kitchen knife, and cut a big wedge for herself. We sat on the couch together while she devoured every morsel. She tried to guess what kind of cake it was with its orange glow. Carrot? Banana? Zucchini? She couldn't guess correctly. When she found out that there were sweet potatoes in the cake, Banks said, "I don't even like sweet potatoes, but I love this cake!"

I remember another day when our Aunt Evelyn Gantt brought us a beautiful jar of purple jelly—clear purple—and you could see right through it. "Guess what kind of jelly this is, Brenda," she said. Well, I guessed everything I could think of that was purple: blackberries, dewberries, blueberries, muscadines, scuppernong. I couldn't think of another thing. She laughed and, with a proud but loving smile, told me it was made from the hulls of purple hull peas. I suppose you can add sugar to anything and make jelly.

My point is whether you're serving cake like me or sharing jelly like Aunt Evelyn, use what you have—sweet potatoes, hulls, peelings, cores, or bones—and make it delicious. That's what folks did during the Great Depression. Those folks were creative and didn't waste a single thing. We can share what we have just as they did in those days.

POPPY SEED CHICKEN

Bring this meal to a new neighbor or to a friend to brighten their day. It's so good, y'all! Serve it up with white rice and my Sour Cream Cornbread.

5 to 6 boneless skinless chicken breasts
    (cut into bite-size pieces)
2   (10.5-ounce) cans cream of chicken
    soup
1   (16-ounce) container sour cream
1   tablespoon poppy seeds
1   teaspoon garlic powder
1   teaspoon onion powder
½   teaspoon salt
2   sleeves round buttery crackers
    (crushed)
1½ sticks salted butter (melted)
Cooked white rice
Sour Cream Cornbread (recipe on
    page 221)

1. Preheat oven to 350°.
2. In large pot, cover chicken with water and bring to a boil over medium-high heat until cooked completely, about 15 to 18 minutes. Drain in a colander.
3. Mix together soup, sour cream, poppy seeds, garlic powder, onion powder, and salt. Spoon half of the soup mixture into an 11x7-inch ungreased casserole dish. Put the cooked chicken on top of the soup in the casserole dish. Do not stir. Add the remaining soup mixture on top of the chicken.
4. In a bowl, mix the crushed crackers and melted butter. Stir well. Put cracker mixture on top of the casserole.
5. Bake until the casserole is good and hot and the crackers are toasted, 30 to 35 minutes. Serve over rice with Sour Cream Cornbread.

"Yes, the good Lord knew what we needed in this life. So, He gave us arms to hug with, lips to kiss, and a tongue to say, 'I love you.'"

EGG SALAD

Egg salad on white bread cut into triangles is a Southern thing—and we don't trim the crusts off. You will see egg salad served at picnics, front porch gatherings, or church homecomings. Make you some!

8 large eggs
¾ cup mayonnaise
2 stalks celery (finely chopped)
1 teaspoon black pepper
¼ teaspoon salt
⅔ cup sweet pickle relish (drained well)

1. In a boiler, add eggs and cover with water. Bring to a boil over medium heat for 10 minutes. Remove the shells and separate the yolks from the whites.
2. Put the yolks in a medium bowl and mash up well. Add mayonnaise and stir well.
3. Chop the whites into very small pieces and then add to the yolk mixture. Add celery, pepper, salt, and pickle relish. (Make sure the relish is drained well through a tea strainer, or your salad will be way too soupy.) Stir well.

Isabella learns to grate hard-boiled eggs. We believe in starting them early.

BUT RATHER SEEK YE THE KINGDOM OF GOD; AND ALL THESE THINGS SHALL BE ADDED UNTO YOU. —LUKE 12:31, KJV

KITCHEN WISDOM

Shell the hard-boiled eggs by running cold water from the tap over them while removing the shell. This makes it much easier. This recipe yields enough to make a whole platter of sandwiches.

NEIGHBOR SOUP

My Hannah loves helping out a neighbor in need, and this soup is her favorite dish to bring to a sick friend or a new mama who can use a quick meal. She usually puts it in quart-size jars, making it easy to transport and store, and serves it with cornbread or crackers.

1   (4- to 5-pound) whole chicken
13 cups water
2   cups celery (diced)
2   cups carrot (sliced)
1   (1-ounce) envelope dry ranch seasoning
½ teaspoon salt (or more to taste)
1   (10-ounce) package yellow rice

1. Place chicken in a large stockpot. Cover with about 10 cups water. Bring to a boil and cook until tender, about 40 to 50 minutes. Remove chicken from the broth and let cool. Skin, debone, and cut or shred chicken. Set aside.

2. Add celery, carrot, ranch seasoning, and salt to broth. (I also add remaining 2 to 3 cups water.) Allow the vegetables to cook about 6 to 8 minutes. Then, add rice and cook over medium heat at a low boil, uncovered, for about 18 minutes. Remove from heat so rice doesn't continue to cook for too long. Add chicken to soup.

Hannah has always loved hats of any kind.

George and Bay show off their outfits for the Hawaiian gathering at church.

BRENDA'S "USE WHAT YOU HAVE" CASSEROLE

Sometimes, I make a dish from what I have on hand in the pantry and fridge, and it turns out amazing, so I keep the recipe and make it again.

1 (20-ounce) can refried pinto beans
1 cup rice (cooked)
1 large onion (chopped and sautéed)
1 large bell pepper (chopped and sautéed)
1 cup ground beef (cooked)
1 (16-ounce) container sour cream
1 (8-ounce) block pepper Jack cheese (grated)
Several dashes of paprika
Dash of flavor enhancer
Dash of garlic powder
1 (10-ounce) package frozen spinach (thawed and drained)

1. Preheat oven to 350°.
2. Spread beans in a casserole dish.
3. Mix together rice, onion, bell pepper, ground beef, half of sour cream, half of cheese, paprika, flavor enhancer, and garlic powder. Spread beef mixture on top of beans.
4. Layer with spinach, remaining sour cream, and remaining cheese.
5. Bake until hot and cheese is melted, about 30 minutes.

"When your groceries are almost gone, you can make a good dish out of just about anything if you season it right."

Walt and Hannah on Christmas morning. They both had given each other a new hat.

BACON-WRAPPED CHICKEN

*While this chicken may seem really fancy, it's simple to make.
You can make it ahead, keep it in the refrigerator overnight, and bake it just
before serving. It's very satisfying with rice. My friends and I have
been making it since the '70s.*

4   boneless skinless chicken breasts
Salt and black pepper to taste
1   (2.25-ounce) jar dried beef
    (chipped up)
1   pound sliced bacon
1   (10.5-ounce) can cream of chicken
    soup
1   (10.5-ounce) can cream of
    mushroom soup
⅔   cup sour cream

1. Preheat oven to 350°.
2. Fillet each chicken breast in half lengthwise, cutting all the way through, and open and lay flat. Cut off extra fat. Sprinkle each with salt and pepper. Sprinkle each with dried beef. Roll up each chicken fillet and wrap each with 1 or 2 bacon slices. Place wrapped chicken in a greased casserole dish, seam side down.
3. Mix soups and sour cream together and pour over the wrapped chicken.
4. Cover with foil and bake for 1 hour and 20 minutes. Uncover and bake until slightly browned.

Life's Collections

Vintage valentines drew me into collecting them, with their bright colors, rhyming words, pop outs, and cute characters. George and I were in the antiques business for over 20 years. We bought the contents of many old homes. That's where I got most of mine. Folks never threw away their personal valentines because they were given by people who loved them.

CHOCOLATE POUND CAKE

Who doesn't enjoy pound cake? This one is for all the chocolate lovers out there. You can leave it plain or sprinkle it with powdered sugar if you want a fancy touch.

2   sticks salted butter, softened
½   cup shortening
3   cups granulated sugar
5   large eggs (room temperature)
3   cups White Lily all-purpose flour
½   teaspoon baking powder
½   teaspoon salt
6   tablespoons cocoa powder
1   cup whole milk or buttermilk
1   tablespoon vanilla extract
Powdered sugar (optional)

Big Daddy gets a hug from Banks (left). Our grandbabies linger around the table that belonged to George's great-grandparents.

1. Preheat oven to 300°. Grease and flour a tube pan.
2. In a stand mixer, beat butter, shortening, and granulated sugar together until creamy. Beat in eggs, one at a time.
3. In a bowl, mix together flour, baking powder, salt, and cocoa; stir well. Add flour mixture and milk alternately to butter mixture, beating until combined. Mix in vanilla. Pour batter into prepared pan.
4. Bake for about 1 hour and 45 minutes to 2 hours. Dust with powdered sugar, if desired.

KITCHEN WISDOM

Not all ovens are created equal. Sometimes, it might take longer (or less time) for a cake to bake in your oven. A good test to see if it's done is to stick a wooden pick in the center; if it comes out clean, your cake is ready.

CHICKEN BOG

The very first time I ever ate Chicken Bog was in Red Level, Alabama, in the kitchen of Carlene and Mike Anderson. We all sat around the table with the big cook pot right smack in the middle—I think Carlene was trying to tempt me to eat more. It worked! I was ashamed of myself for eating so much. It's like a comfort food—you just have to go back for more.

2 tablespoons olive oil
1 pound smoked sausage links (sliced into ½-inch rounds)
1 medium yellow onion (chopped)
2 cloves garlic (chopped)
1 (4- to 5-pound) whole chicken
1½ cups long-grain white rice
1 cup chopped celery
1 teaspoon salt
1 teaspoon black pepper

1. In a skillet, add olive oil and sausage and cook until lightly browned. Add onion and garlic to sausage and cook. Set aside.

2. In a large pot, place chicken with water to cover over medium-high heat. Cook until tender. Remove chicken from broth in the pot. Skin, debone, and shred chicken. Set aside (about 4 cups). Reserve chicken broth.

3. In the same pot, add 5 cups reserved broth, rice, celery, salt, and pepper. Cook over medium heat until the rice is tender, about 25 to 30 minutes. When rice gets tender, add shredded chicken and the sausage mixture to the pot. If the mixture seems too thick, add some more chicken broth. Serve with cornbread topped with pepper jelly.

Carlene and Mike Anderson with George and me. They're really good friends that have now moved to Texas. Some of our best little moments were spent with Carlene and Mike.

ITALIAN VEGGIE BEEF SOUP

I don't know where this soup got its name, but it's full of good vegetables and herbs. This is one of Anna's favorite recipes to share with friends in need.

1½   pounds lean ground beef
1   medium onion (diced)
1   (10-ounce) bag shredded carrots
3   stalks celery (strings removed and chopped)
3   cloves garlic (minced)
1   (28-ounce) can petite diced tomatoes
1   (15-ounce) can crushed tomatoes
1   teaspoon dried basil
1   teaspoon dried oregano
1   teaspoon dried thyme
2   cups water
Salt and black pepper to taste
2   (15-ounce) cans navy beans (undrained)
½   pound ditalini or small shell pasta

1. In a large pot, cook beef over medium heat until browned. Drain and return beef to pan.
2. Add onion, carrot, and celery to beef and cook over medium heat until vegetables start to become tender. Add garlic, all tomatoes, basil, oregano, and thyme, stirring to combine. Stir in 2 cups water. Season with salt and pepper. Stir in beans. Cover and simmer over medium-low heat, stirring occasionally, until all ingredients are tender.
3. In a separate pot, cook pasta. (Don't overcook pasta; you will want it to be a little firm.) Add cooked pasta to soup during the last 5 minutes before serving or add the pasta to individual serving bowls, as desired.

KITCHEN WISDOM

Anna prefers to use navy beans for this soup, but you can use kidney, black, or great northern. This dish can be made a day ahead, and it's wonderful to give away. I use empty pickle jars to store leftover soup and to carry the soup to a friend in need. So, save your big pickle jars; they will come in handy!

BLACK SKILLET APPLE PIE

*Sometimes, you need to put together a dessert for a sick friend.
This fuss-free pie combines brown sugar, butter, and sweet, crispy apples with
refrigerated piecrusts in a cast-iron skillet. It's so quick! You can be at that
neighbor's door with this pie and a smile in no time at all.*

5   medium Granny Smith apples
½   stick salted butter
1¼   cups light brown sugar
2   tablespoons White Lily all-purpose
      flour
2   refrigerated piecrusts
¾   cup granulated sugar
1   teaspoon ground cinnamon
1   large egg white

1. Preheat oven to 350°.
2. Peel apples and cut into thick slices. Set aside.
3. Put butter in microwave-safe bowl and melt, about 30 seconds. Add ½ cup brown sugar and flour to hot melted butter and stir well. Pour brown sugar mixture in the bottom of a 10-inch cast-iron skillet. Put 1 piecrust over brown sugar mixture in skillet.
4. In a bowl, toss together apples, ½ cup granulated sugar, remaining ¾ cup brown sugar, and cinnamon. Put apple mixture into piecrust in skillet. Place remaining piecrust on top of the apple mixture and pinch the two crusts together using your fingers.
5. Whisk egg white really well with a fork. Brush egg white on top of crust. Sprinkle remaining 4 tablespoons granulated sugar on top of egg wash. Make a small cut in the top of the pie to let steam escape.
6. Bake until crust is browned, about 50 minutes to 1 hour.

You can't have too many cast-iron skillets!

William and Dallas share a little moment outdoors.

CHEESE STRAW COOKIES

Golden coins of Cheddar cheese make a great snack or party food. You can even package them in pretty containers with a ribbon and give them as gifts.

1   stick salted butter (room temperature)
1½   cups White Lily all-purpose flour (unsifted)
Pinch of salt
¼   teaspoon ground red pepper
2¾   cups grated sharp Cheddar cheese (room temperature)
1   teaspoon water

1. Preheat oven to 350°. Lightly grease a baking sheet with vegetable oil. (Do not use cooking spray.)
2. In a stand mixer, mix together butter, flour, salt, red pepper, and cheese. Knead until mixture is smooth. Add in 1 teaspoon water, a little at a time, as needed to make mixture stick together.

3. Form cheese mixture into small walnut-size balls. Flatten with your hand or the bottom of a glass to make a small cookie shape. Place on greased baking sheet.
4. Bake for 25 to 35 minutes. Cookies should be crispy, depending on your oven. Let cool and then store in an airtight container.

"Doing what you say you will do is called being dependable."

Life's Little Moments

We've all been sick with a high fever at one time or another. The touch of a loving hand on our brow, some hot chicken soup to eat, a cool cloth on our forehead, or, as a child, being rocked in our mama's arms—all these are important little moments. They bring security, assurance, and hope to the sick.

BLUEBERRY CRUNCH

You can use any fruit pie filling you like, including strawberry, apple, or mixed berry. It is wonderful no matter what flavor I pick.

1   (21-ounce) can blueberry pie filling
1   (20-ounce) can crushed pineapple (undrained)
1   (15.25-ounce) box yellow or white cake mix
1½ cups pecans (chopped)
1½ sticks salted margarine (melted)
Ice cream

1. Preheat oven to 350°. Grease a 13x9-inch baking dish.
2. Pour pie filling and pineapple into the prepared dish. Sprinkle cake mix over fruit. Top with pecans. Pour melted margarine on top.
3. Bake until cake is done and fruit is bubbly, about 45 minutes to 1 hour. Serve with ice cream.

Love those hugs. I had to get all of the hugs I could from Cape when she was a baby because she is stingy with them now.

Bay and William share a snack and a little playfulness at the table.

chapter 4

ONE-POT WONDERS

TRAIL RIDERS

On our first family vacation last year, we found ourselves all excited to be in the gorgeous Montana mountains. Thoughts of the trip had been lingering in our minds for months. The anticipation was kind of like waiting for Christmas; we thought it would never get here. Bay, Isabella, Banks, and Cape had their minds set on buying some new western clothing—maybe a hat, a belt, fancy pants, or a piece of turquoise jewelry. William, on the other hand, is like any other 15-year-old boy. If he has a T-shirt, comfortable shorts, and tennis shoes, he's a happy camper. Boys are so much easier to raise than girls! But on this day, shopping would have to wait. We had planned a mountain trail ride on, sure enough, real Montana horses!

Gathered in the corral, the horses looked beautiful with the sun gleaming on their shiny coats. They were fat and happy horses and ready for trail riding. There were some horses with deep colors of brown and black; some were creamy white or had touches of gray, and the beautiful spotted Appaloosas were standing ready to ride. We all were looking forward to saddling up, but I have to admit that I was a little anxious. When I was a teen, I'd fallen off a horse. The saddle was not secured, so when I put my foot in the stirrup, the saddle and I both slid underneath the belly of the horse. Have you ever been there? It's a real fright to look up at the underside of a big workhorse! On another occasion, I climbed on a horse rightly named Jughead because he was crazy. You never knew what he might do. I got on him bareback, and he went flying across the pasture at the speed of light. Being so scared, I jumped off that crazy Jughead. He kept running straight ahead, and I ran in the opposite direction—home.

In Montana, all 10 of us had to weigh in before the ride, and one of our crew, my son, Dallas, weighed over the 225-pound limit. Now, we were really nervous! We all held our breath as William, my teenage grandson, got on the scales. He came very close to the limit, weighing in at 223 pounds. Good thing he didn't eat that extra biscuit at breakfast! We all had to laugh knowing this would be William's first and last horse ride. Surely, a growing 15-year-old boy would be over the limit in just a few months.

The stable workers matched each rider with the perfect horse and lined them up with Hannah and Anna between the children and Walt at the tail end. They followed the trail master's lead up to the steep mountain edge. Soon, they were out of sight on the trail under the canopy of huge Montana trees.

Not wanting Dallas to be alone, I was more than happy to stay back with him. He parked our vehicle in the lot so the sun would be at our backs while we waited two hours for the rest of our family to return. Now, you might be thinking—this is awful that Dallas and Brenda didn't get to go on the trail. Well, God always has a better plan. You know, He can change ashes into beauty. Turns out that this was one of my favorite memories of our family vacation. With the car windows rolled down, the mountain breezes blowing, ground squirrels running from under an old wagon wheel, a big white-faced bull staring at us from his pasture, and horses that were left behind grazing, Dallas and I were at peace. We talked about the Lord, our plans, special memories, all the family, the kids, and, of course, my George—wishing that he, too, could have been here with us. We reminisced, laughed, and just had an all-around great time being together. The good Lord knew we needed this priceless moment together.

The riders finally returned with sore butts, tales to tell, hungry stomachs, and thankful-to-be-alive attitudes. Hannah's words to me were: "Mama, I'm glad you didn't go. You would have had a heart attack on those scary, rocky cliffs. You're not one to put your trust in a horse, that's for sure."

"Each of us has special gifts, talents, and abilities to be used for the betterment of others; if not used correctly, our society will fall apart."

BROCCOLI CHOWDER

———— ◆ ————

Broccoli and cheese make such a good combination. If you're lucky enough to have some of this chowder left over, you need to know that it will naturally become thicker the next day. Just add some water and stir it up until it reaches the consistency you like.

3   bunches fresh broccoli
4½   cups water
1   stick salted butter
2   cups whole milk
5   tablespoons White Lily all-purpose flour
1   (8-ounce) package processed cheese product (cut into cubes)
¾   teaspoon salt
Grated Cheddar cheese

1. Cut broccoli florets into small pieces. Leave stems whole. In a large stockpot, combine 4 cups water, florets, and stems. Bring to a boil and cook until very tender. Remove stems and discard. Using the side of a spoon, chop florets and leave in the remaining water. Add butter and continue to simmer. Add milk.

2. Mix together flour and remaining ½ cup water in a small bowl until there are no lumps. Slowly add flour mixture to soup while stirring continuously until mixed.

3. Add processed cheese product and stir well until it melts. Add salt. Now, it is ready to eat. Top each serving with a little grated Cheddar cheese.

Hannah and I painted her bedroom hot pink. We did whatever we could to make Hannah happy.

Isabella, George, and Cape on vacation in Helen, Georgia

LASAGNA

—————◆—————

This takes a little time to prepare, but it's worth it. Everybody enjoys a good lasagna on a cold winter's night. Those with a hearty appetite love it!

2 pounds ground chuck
1 large onion (chopped)
2 cloves garlic (minced)
2 (15-ounce) cans tomato sauce
1 (15-ounce) can whole tomatoes
1 tablespoon garlic powder
1 tablespoon dried oregano
1 tablespoon dried Italian seasoning
1 tablespoon salt
1 tablespoon black pepper
9 lasagna noodles (cooked)
3 (8-ounce) packages sliced mozzarella cheese
1 (24-ounce) container cottage cheese
3 cups grated Cheddar cheese
Grated Parmesan cheese

1. Preheat oven to 350°.
2. In a large pot, cook ground chuck, onion, and garlic until the meat is browned. Drain in a colander.
3. In the same pot, combine drained beef mixture, tomato sauce, whole tomatoes, and all seasonings. Cover and simmer sauce over medium heat for 1 hour or longer.
4. Grease a 13x9-inch casserole pan.
5. To assemble in prepared pan, layer ingredients in this order: 1½ cups sauce, spreading to edges. Layer 3 noodles, one-third of sauce, one-third of mozzarella slices, half of cottage cheese, one-third of Cheddar, 3 noodles, one-third of sauce, one-third of mozzarella slices, one-third of Cheddar, remaining cottage cheese, remaining 3 noodles, remaining sauce, remaining mozzarella slices, and remaining Cheddar. Sprinkle with Parmesan.
6. Bake until bubbly, 30 to 45 minutes.

Anna in the Bahamas, swimming with the pigs on CocoCay

STUMP JUMPIN' SAUSAGE

Hannah created this dish when Walt was stump jumpin' on the campaign trail for district attorney. It's easy and affordable, and it can sit for hours over low heat on the stovetop for everyone to eat in shifts. Hannah even served it one night for a campaign function at a local restaurant. It's perfect over Creamy Cheese Grits on page 103 or white rice.

1   pound smoked sausage links (sliced into thin rounds)
2   tablespoons water
2   stalks celery (chopped)
1   medium onion (diced)
1   tablespoon minced garlic
1½ cups chicken broth
1   (28-ounce) can petite diced tomatoes
1   (16-ounce) can pinto beans (drained)
Creole seasoning (to taste)
1   tablespoon cornstarch

1. In a skillet (not cast iron), cook sausage and 2 tablespoons water over medium-low heat until water has cooked out and sausage is starting to brown. Remove any grease that has formed.

2. In the same skillet, add celery, onion, and garlic to sausage and continue to cook over medium-low heat until vegetables become tender. Add chicken broth and scrape the bottom of the skillet to get all the goodie in the juice. Then, add tomatoes and beans. Season with Creole seasoning, depending on how spicy you like it. Simmer over low heat for at least 30 minutes.

3. In a coffee cup, whisk together cornstarch and just a little water to make a thin paste. Stir cornstarch mixture into sausage mixture and cook until thickened. Stir occasionally. Serve over cheese grits or rice.

Walt loves being on the water.

"You can't see the wind, but we feel it against our skin and see its mighty power. We can't see God, but we feel Him in our hearts and see His mighty works."

CREAMY CHEESE GRITS

Adding whipping cream and cream cheese turns this dish into a special accompaniment for breakfast, lunch, or dinner. Make sure you whisk the grits quickly when you add them to the liquid so they don't clump.

2 cups low-sodium chicken broth
3 cups water
1 teaspoon salt
1½ cups old-fashioned grits
2 cups heavy whipping cream
½ stick salted butter (room temperature)
1 (4-ounce) package cream cheese (room temperature)

1. In a boiler, combine chicken broth and 2 cups water. Bring to a boil. Add salt.

Whisk in grits. (You must whisk constantly so there will not be lumps.) Immediately reduce heat to medium-low and simmer, uncovered, for 7 to 8 minutes. (Grits will be getting thick at this point.)

2. Add remaining 1 cup water and cream. Add butter. Allow grits mixture to heat back up over medium-low heat and continue to cook, uncovered, for 20 to 30 minutes, stirring frequently. Add cream cheese at the end and stir well until melted. Serve immediately. Serve with more butter.

— Life's Little Moments

On hot summer days, we would put a small, blue plastic swimming pool on the green grass in our front yard. The grandbabies loved splashing, screaming, and enjoying the cool water. One day, George and I were watching them from the front porch swing. Wouldn't you know it, they talked Big Daddy into getting in the pool of water with them. Mind you, the pool was maybe 5 feet across, and his 6-foot body lying in the water left little room for the five young'uns. Somehow, they all played in the water at one time. What a sight to behold! It was a little moment we will never forget. We laughed until we couldn't laugh anymore.

FLO'S EASY CHICKEN GUMBO

Growing up, my brothers and I would get off the school bus and run down the driveway to the kitchen door. There, my mama, Flo Hicks, would have a huge pot of gumbo and a big skillet of cornbread ready for us. I don't know why, but we were always starving after school. Daddy worked the 3 p.m. to 11 p.m. shift at Hunt Oil Company. Mama would often cook a big pot of something to take to him for supper at work. We would all pile into the car, drive to Hunt Oil, and visit with Daddy while he ate. Mama always thought of others, especially Daddy and her kids.

1 (4- to 5-pound) whole chicken
1 bay leaf
2 (14.5-ounce) cans diced tomatoes
2 onions (chopped)
2 (10-ounce) packages frozen cut okra
1 cup long-grain white rice
Salt and black pepper to taste

1. Cut chicken into pieces. Place in a large boiler and cover with water. Use a lot of water (about 12 cups) as this will be your broth. Add bay leaf and boil until chicken is very tender, 45 minutes to 1 hour. Discard the bay leaf.
2. Remove chicken from broth. Skin, debone, and chop up chicken.
3. Place chicken back into broth. Add tomatoes and onion, and simmer about 15 minutes. Add okra and cook until tender and done. Add rice and cook until tender. Season with salt and pepper.

My parents, Flo and Cecil Hicks, loved the beach. Every year, we vacationed at the beach; Mama would blister, and Daddy would tan.

Cape wears a sombrero and makes a mess with some whipped cream.

CHEESE CHICKEN

*This dish of melted cheese over chicken breasts is very comforting.
Serve it over rice with a side of broccoli, asparagus, or green beans for a
well-balanced meal. It's great for a potluck supper, too.*

2   pounds boneless skinless chicken
    breasts
Salt and black pepper
White Lily all-purpose flour
2 to 3 tablespoons oil
1   (10.5-ounce) can cream of chicken
    soup
1   (8-ounce) container sour cream
1 to 1½ cups whole milk
1   (8-ounce) package sliced Muenster
    cheese

1. Preheat oven to 350°.
2. Pat chicken breasts dry with a paper
towel. If they are small, leave as is. If
large chicken breasts, then cut into 2 or
more pieces. Season with salt and pepper
and then dredge in flour.
3. In a frying pan, cook chicken in oil
over medium-low heat until both sides
are golden. Place chicken in a greased
casserole dish. (Chicken should fill the
dish and fit tightly with little to no room
between pieces.)
4. In a bowl, combine soup and sour
cream. Add milk and stir until smooth,
about the consistency of medium
pancake batter. Season with salt and
pepper to taste. Set aside.
5. Place cheese slices over chicken in the
casserole dish. Pour soup mixture over
chicken. Cover with a lid or foil.
6. Bake until it is bubbly throughout,
about 30 minutes.

Anna loves one-pot meals. They make life easier with her work schedule.

KITCHEN WISDOM

If you can't find Muenster cheese, you can substitute Havarti, Gouda, provolone, or any
soft, mild cheese. Or you could even use Cheddar cheese.

WALT'S CHILI ALABAMA

Walt likes to try his hand at cooking every now and then, and he is quite good at it. One of his best recipes is this meaty chili that includes beef tips, ground beef, and bacon. But the best part is the drizzle of honey at the end, which brings out all of the rich flavors.

1 pound beef tips
1 pound ground beef
½ onion (chopped)
½ green bell pepper (chopped)
1 (15-ounce) can tomato sauce
½ cup water
2 (15.5-ounce) cans dark red kidney beans (1 can drained)
2 teaspoons chili powder
1 teaspoon paprika
½ teaspoon dried oregano
¼ teaspoon salt
¼ teaspoon black pepper
8 slices bacon

Honey to drizzle
Grated Cheddar cheese
Sour cream (optional)

1. Brown beef tips and ground beef in separate skillets. Drain.
2. In a large pot, combine all beef, onion, and bell pepper. Cook over medium heat for 10 minutes. Add tomato sauce, ½ cup water, beans, and all spices. Cover and simmer for 35 minutes.
3. In the meantime, fry bacon and crumble.
4. When all is done, serve chili in bowls and top with bacon, honey, and cheese. Add sour cream, if desired.

Walt supports George as he is inducted into the Andalusia High School Football Hall of Fame.

William helps me prepare a holiday turkey that's about as big as he is.

CHICKEN CABBAGE SOUP

Being on a diet is hard work. It seems like we just can't satisfy our hunger.
Well, you can enjoy this soup because it's so good without all the calories.

1 (4- to 5-pound) whole chicken
2 (1.4-ounce) envelopes dry vegetable soup mix
8 small green onions (white and green parts chopped)
5 stalks celery (chopped, leaves and all)
4 carrots (sliced into rounds)
3 cloves garlic (minced)
2 large onions (chopped)
1 red bell pepper (chopped)
½ large green bell pepper (chopped)
½ medium head cabbage (cut into cubes)
2 (14.5-ounce) cans petite diced tomatoes
1 teaspoon salt
1 teaspoon paprika
1 teaspoon dried basil

1. Place chicken in a large stockpot. Cover with water and bring to a boil. Add soup mix to pot and simmer until chicken is tender and cooked. Remove chicken from broth and let cool. Skin and debone chicken. Set aside the dark meat in a bowl. Wrap the white meat in plastic wrap to save in the fridge for another day. (You can use it to make chicken salad.)

2. Skim the grease off the top of broth in the pot and discard. Add the remaining ingredients to broth. Cover and cook until carrot and cabbage are tender. Some water can be added to soup as it cooks, if needed.

3. Chop dark meat into cubes and add to the soup.

A pleasant visit with my college friends in Orange Beach, Alabama.

Life's Collections

When I get together with my college girlfriends at the beach, we often walk at the water's edge early in the morning and gather all the pretty shells we see. We can't resist a pretty shell. I can blow a conch shell loud and clear. Can you?

RED BEANS AND RICE

———◆———

Here's a tried-and-true recipe for a well-known Louisiana dish. Serve it with my Buttermilk Cornbread on page 217 and sop up some of the liquid with it. Make it as spicy as you like with Creole seasoning and add some heat with red pepper.

1	pound dried kidney beans
6	cups water
2	bay leaves
1	tablespoon dried parsley
1	teaspoon dried thyme
1	teaspoon Creole seasoning
1	teaspoon salt
½	teaspoon ground red pepper
1	pound andouille or kielbasa sausage (sliced into rounds)
¼	cup olive oil
1	large onion (chopped)
1	green bell pepper (chopped)
2	stalks celery (chopped)
3	cloves garlic (minced)
2	cups long-grain white rice
Green onions (as garnish)	

1. Rinse beans and soak in water overnight. On the next morning, drain beans.
2. In a large stockpot, add 6 cups water, beans, and all spices and herbs. Bring to a boil and then simmer for 2 hours and 30 minutes, adding more water as needed.
3. While beans are simmering, cook sausage in olive oil in a skillet. Remove sausage, leaving drippings in the pan, and set aside.
4. Sauté onion, bell pepper, and celery in the sausage drippings. Right before the onion is about finished, add garlic and sauté 1 to 2 minutes. Add vegetables and sausage to bean mixture. Let simmer.
5. When the beans are tender and ready, discard bay leaves. Cook rice according to package instructions. Serve the red beans over a bed of rice and garnish with green onions, if desired.

"If you don't keep moving and doing, you will rust; then, you will be useless to everyone, including yourself."

——— KITCHEN WISDOM ———

You must keep adding more water during the cooking process because the beans will quickly soak up the water. If not, that means burnt-up beans and no supper!

chapter 5

FALL IS IN THE AIR

SWEET POTATO PLANTING

The day had finally come. Uncle Pickens Gantt was at our garden at daybreak. He was in his late 80s and lived just down the road from us. Uncle Pickens treated me like his very own daughter and George like his son. He and Aunt Evelyn never had grandchildren of their own, so our children, Dallas and Hannah, became theirs. Aunt Evelyn even took Hannah to get her driver's permit. She also took Dallas to get his driver's license and let him take the driving test in her Cadillac. They loved our little family, and we were blessed to have them in ours. Whether we were shelling butter beans, shucking corn, or building our house, Uncle Pickens was always ready to help. But, this day in the garden was special. We were learning how to plant sweet potatoes. George had laid the rows with the tractor the day before—long and straight with the rich soil standing up at least 12 inches high in each. Uncle Pickens walked over to the wood's edge, took out his pocketknife, and cut a tree limb about the thickness of your finger and over a yard long. At the end of the limb was a V-shape where it had split into two smaller limbs. He showed us how to put a little green potato shoot in between the "V" and push it right down into the very top of the hill of soil. When we finished planting, we turned around to look at the long row of freshly planted sweet potato shoots. Harvesttime finally came. All three of us dug up the potatoes—baskets and baskets of them. Uncle Pickens said to store them in a dark, cool place. Since we always slept in a very cold bedroom with no heat, storing them under our bed in shallow cardboard boxes was a perfect place. I know one thing for sure: older people have so much knowledge and are always ready to share it. Uncle Pickens has passed on now. I think of him often and wish he were still here to help at harvesttime.

He would have enjoyed teaching our grandchildren a thing or two. He lived his life helping others, and, y'all, we should do the same.

"We've all heard the old saying, 'Bloom where you are planted.' Are you root-bound, dried up, stunted, or wilted? Start blooming!"

APPLE CIDER

—◆—

Nothing says fall like apple cider. It makes your house smell so wonderful while you're making it. It's warm to the body as you slowly sip it down.

½ gallon apple cider (refrigerated)
1 medium orange (wash and score the skin before you slice)
⅓ cup pineapple juice
3 whole cinnamon sticks
9 whole cloves
⅓ cup light brown sugar (firmly packed)

1. Pour cider into a stockpot. Add orange slices, pineapple juice, cinnamon sticks, cloves, and brown sugar. Heat over medium heat until mixture starts to roll but not a hard boil.
2. Reduce heat to low and let simmer for about 45 minutes. Strain solids and serve hot.

Fall is in the air with pumpkin carving and sunflowers.

SLOTHFULNESS CASTETH INTO A DEEP SLEEP; AND AN IDLE SOUL SHALL SUFFER HUNGER. —PROVERBS 19:15, KJV

KITCHEN WISDOM

Cut some apple slices really thin to float in your cider and serve it with some cinnamon sticks on the side for stirring. If you want to bring it to a tailgate or a party, keep the cider warm in a slow cooker or an insulated container. Everyone enjoys a warm beverage when there is a chill in the air.

CARAMEL TOPPING SAUCE

———◆———

Made from five ingredients, you'll enjoy this sauce over and over again.

½ stick salted butter
1½ cups light brown sugar
⅔ cup light corn syrup
⅔ cup sour cream
1 cup coarsely chopped pecans

1. In a small saucepan, melt butter over medium heat. Stir in brown sugar and corn syrup. Cook, stirring constantly, over medium heat until mixture comes to a boil. Remove from heat.
2. Stir in sour cream and pecans. Stir sauce before serving. Serve warm or cold drizzled over mocha pecan ice cream or vanilla ice cream. Refrigerate leftover sauce.

Hannah and Walt

"Keep this sauce on hand for drizzling over ice cream and other sweets. It's addictive!"

William, Big Daddy, and Banks play Scrabble at the kitchen table.

KITCHEN WISDOM

After storing leftover Caramel Topping Sauce in the refrigerator, it will be hard. To serve, dip out the amount you want to use, soften it in the microwave, stir, and enjoy!

15 BEAN SOUP

You just have to serve this soup with a slice of onion, saltines, and iced tea. You don't need anything else! This soup is a complete meal. It's high in protein, cheap, and delicious.

1   (20-ounce) package dry 15 bean soup mix
2   quarts water
Salt and black pepper to taste
1   large onion (diced)
1   tablespoon vegetable oil
2   (14.5-ounce) cans petite diced tomatoes (undrained)
1   pound smoked sausage links (cut into rounds, fried, and drained)
1   tablespoon Cajun seasoning

1. Wash beans and add to a stockpot filled with 2 quarts water. Season with salt and pepper. Bring to a boil over medium-high heat and cook until beans are almost done. (The beans will soak up the water, so a little more water will need to be added as you go along.)
2. Sauté onion in oil. Add onion mixture to bean mixture.
3. Add in tomatoes, sausage, and Cajun seasoning. Finish cooking until beans are tender, about 1 hour.

> NO MAN HATH SEEN GOD AT ANY TIME. IF WE LOVE ONE ANOTHER,
> GOD DWELLETH IN US, AND HIS LOVE IS PERFECTED IN US.
> —1 JOHN 4:12, KJV

HOT SANDWICHES

You'll get lots of oohs and aahs over these satisfying sandwiches.
Serve these with soup, and you'll have the perfect light lunch.

1   loaf good crusty bread (like
    sourdough or French)
Mayonnaise to taste
Dijon mustard to taste
Sliced Colby-Jack cheese
1   avocado (sliced)
1   tomato (sliced)
Salt and black pepper to taste
Garlic-herb seasoning to taste
½   pound sliced smoked turkey or
    deli ham
Salted butter (room temperature)

1. Preheat oven to 400°.
2. Slice bread to desired thickness for sandwiches and slather inside with mayonnaise and mustard. Assemble each sandwich in this order: cheese, avocado, tomato, seasonings, and meat. (Make sure tomato is in the center so bread doesn't become soggy.)
3. Butter the outside of bread on both sides of the sandwiches. Place on a baking sheet.
4. Bake for about 7 minutes. Turn sandwiches to other side and bake for 7 minutes more. The sandwiches should be toasty and the cheese melted.

Uncle Pickens Gantt always wore his hat cocked over to one side because he had one bad eye that was sensitive to light, and he tried to protect it.

Cape, Isabella, Banks, William, and I pull up turnip roots that we grew.

STUFFED BUTTERNUT SQUASH

You can make this squash ahead of time and put it in the refrigerator overnight. When you are ready to serve it, bring it to room temperature and then bake it in the oven until the cheese is all gooey and melted.

1   (8-inch) butternut squash
2   tablespoons olive oil
⅓   (16-ounce) package ground sausage
¼   green bell pepper (chopped)
2   green onions (chopped)
1   teaspoon dried Italian seasoning
¾   teaspoon dried thyme
¾   teaspoon garlic powder
¾   cup cooked white rice
¼   cup grated sharp Cheddar cheese
¼   cup grated Parmesan cheese

1. Preheat oven to 400°.
2. Cut the squash in half lengthwise. Scrape out seeds and strings. Score the inside flesh with a sharp knife. Rub olive oil on flesh of each half of squash. Cover the bottom of a baking dish with foil. Lay each squash half, cut side down, in the dish.
3. Bake for 45 to 50 minutes. Check tenderness with a metal skewer. Let cool for about 15 minutes.
4. While the squash is baking, cook sausage, bell pepper, and green onion in a skillet over medium heat until sausage is done. Remove from heat. Add spices, rice, Cheddar, and half of Parmesan to sausage mixture and stir well.
5. When the squash is ready, scrape out the flesh, being careful not to tear the sides of the squash. Add the flesh to the sausage mixture. Stir well. Fill each squash half with the sausage mixture. Top with the remaining Parmesan. Lightly tent the squash with foil.
6. Bake until stuffing is hot and cheese has melted. Serve hot right out of the oven.

Dallas, Isabella, and William are dressed and ready for the hunt.

SMOTHERED FRIED STEAK

———◆———

Before you fry this up, you've got to tenderize the meat. I use the top end of a bottle and just pound it all over the steak on both sides. This dish is delicious with some of my Sautéed Onions.

1   (2- to 3-pound) boneless top round
    steak
Salt and black pepper
1   cup White Lily all-purpose flour
⅓   cup vegetable oil
2   cups water
Sautéed Onions (recipe at right)

1. Lay the steak on your chopping board. Pound both sides with a meat mallet or the top end of a bottle. Cut the steak into serving sizes. Season with salt and pepper.
2. Put flour on a large plate, and coat steak pieces in flour until all pieces are done. Leave the flour on the plate.
3. In a deep skillet, heat the oil over medium-high heat. When oil gets hot, put as many steak pieces in skillet as you can without overlapping. Fry fast on one side until brown, then turn and fry on the other side until brown. Continue until all pieces are browned. Put the steak on a plate and set aside. Leave oil in the skillet.
4. To make the gravy, use oil left in the skillet. (Do not use another skillet; you need all the goodie that is in the bottom of the skillet.) Using the flour left on the plate, measure out about 5 tablespoons. (If there is not enough, simply get more.) Add the flour to oil in the skillet and cook over medium heat, using a spatula to scrape the bottom of the skillet. When flour mixture turns a medium brown, add 2 cups water, stirring constantly with a

whisk. (You may have to add a little bit more water if the gravy seems too thick.) Season with salt and pepper.
5. Reduce the heat to low. Add steak pieces back into the gravy in the skillet and cook for at least 30 to 40 minutes. Top with Sautéed Onions.

SAUTÈED ONIONS

——◆——

4   large sweet onions
½   stick salted butter
Salt and black pepper to taste

1. Peel and cut onions in half and then cut into thin slices. Don't add salt and pepper to the onions at the start of cooking. Salt pulls out liquid and that makes the onions not as good.
2. In a skillet, melt butter over medium heat. Immediately add sliced onions. Stir onions on bottom of pan and bring them to the top so that butter will be on every piece. Cook, stirring occasionally, until the onions are tender and caramelized.
3. Now, sprinkle on salt and pepper. Serve onions as a topping on hamburgers, steaks, and hot dogs or stir into gravy.

CREAM OF TOMATO SOUP

We enjoy this soup on a cold winter night with a grilled cheese sandwich. Glory! You can't beat that with a hoe handle!

⅓ cup sweet onion (minced)
6 tablespoons salted butter
1 teaspoon fresh garlic (finely minced)
1 (28-ounce) can crushed tomatoes
1 cup whole milk
1½ cups heavy whipping cream
¼ teaspoon dried basil
Grated Parmesan cheese

1. In a stockpot, sauté onion and butter over medium heat until soft and tender. Add garlic and cook over medium-low heat for 1 minute. Add tomatoes to the onion mixture. Stir in milk and cook over medium-low heat. Add whipping cream. Stir and continue to cook over medium-low heat. Add basil. Top with Parmesan when serving.

Cape, Isabella, William, Bay, and Banks—my pretty little pumpkins carving pumpkins

PUMPKIN SPICE LATTE

Banks is always inventing new recipes. This is one she made at my house on a cool fall day. It is delicious! We put lots of real whipped cream on top of ours. Why not?

¼   teaspoon pumpkin pie spice
¼   teaspoon ground cinnamon
¼   teaspoon ground nutmeg
¾   cup heavy whipping cream
2   tablespoons sugar
1   cup whole milk
¼   teaspoon vanilla extract
2   cups brewed coffee
2   tablespoons maple syrup

1. In a bowl, mix pumpkin pie spice, cinnamon, and nutmeg.
2. In a stand mixer, beat whipping cream and sugar until soft peaks form, making a cold foam.
3. Heat milk and vanilla to an almost boil.
4. Take two mugs and fill each with 1 cup coffee. Then, add 1 tablespoon maple syrup in each mug. Finally, add the steamed milk mixture and spice mixture. Mix all together and top with a dollop of whipped cream. Sprinkle a little extra pumpkin pie spice on top, if you'd like.

Big Daddy and Banks

ONION PIE

———— ◆ ————

This pie is a classic Southern dish, especially when sweet Vidalia onions are in season. Serve it for brunch after church on Sundays or as a light supper with a green salad.

1   Pie Paw Piecrust (recipe at right)
4   slices bacon
3   very large, sweet onions (sliced)
3   tablespoons salted butter
4   large eggs
3   tablespoons White Lily self-rising flour
¼   cup whole milk
Salt and black pepper to taste
2   cups grated Cheddar cheese

1. Preheat oven to 350°.
2. Bake the piecrust until partially done.
3. In a skillet, fry the bacon. Crumble and set aside.
4. Sauté the onion in butter until light brown, stirring often. Set aside.
5. Beat the eggs. Add flour and whisk well until no lumps. Add milk. Set aside.
6. In a large bowl, mix onion, egg mixture, salt, pepper, and half of the cheese. Pour mixture into crust. Sprinkle remaining cheese on top.
7. Bake until soft firm, about 30 to 35 minutes. Do not overcook. Add bacon to top of pie as soon as you take it out of the oven. Let cool for 5 or 10 minutes and serve warm.

PIE PAW PIECRUST

———— ◆ ————

You can use this recipe for all kinds of pies. Don't add the milk until the last part and only a little at a time because you may not need it all.

1½   cups White Lily all-purpose flour
2   tablespoons sugar
½   teaspoon salt
½   cup vegetable oil
3½   tablespoons whole milk

1. Preheat oven to 375°.
2. Mix flour, sugar, salt, and oil directly into an ungreased pie plate. Stir well.
3. Slowly add milk, 1 teaspoon at a time, and mold the dough. (Rarely do I use all the milk. Put in the milk a little at a time. If the dough seems a little sticky, add a tad more flour. If the dough seems a little dry, add a tad of milk.) When you reach the desired consistency, press the dough evenly into the pie plate.
4. Bake an empty crust for 20 to 25 minutes. For a filled crust, bake at the direction of the pie recipe.

WHITE CHICKEN CHILI

In the crisp fall, when the trees are becoming bare and everything is frosty outside, put on a pot of this chili. It'll warm you up! Serve it with crackers or a slice of warm cornbread. Be sure to share it!

1 medium onion (diced)
2 tablespoons olive oil
2 pounds bone-in chicken or 1 rotisserie chicken (skinned and deboned)
5½ cups chicken broth
2 (15-ounce) cans black beans or navy beans (drained)
1 (15.25-ounce) can whole sweet corn (drained)
2 (4-ounce) cans diced green chiles
3 cloves garlic (minced)
1 tablespoon ground cumin
1 tablespoon dried oregano
Salt and black pepper to taste

1. In a large pot, sauté onion in oil over medium heat until softened.
2. Add chicken and broth to pot. Bring to a boil. Reduce heat and cover. Simmer for 20 minutes for rotisserie chicken or 40 minutes for raw chicken. If using raw chicken, cook until tender. Remove and debone chicken and add meat back to pot.
3. Add beans, corn, chiles, garlic, cumin, and oregano. Simmer for 15 to 20 minutes. Season with salt and pepper.

Life's Little Moments

On dark fall nights when all the leaves have fallen to the ground, our children and our grandchildren love lying on a blanket under the stars. With its wonder and beauty, the night sky is somehow magical to us all. We talk, listen to the whip-poor-wills, and cuddle with our legs draped across whoever is beside us. Owls sing to us, and we see an occasional shooting star. It's free and beautiful. Live each little moment, y'all.

FRENCH ONION SOUP

Any time we go out to eat in a fancy restaurant, Cape always orders French onion soup. One particular night, she said, "Big Mama, I want you to learn how to make this soup." Being the Big Mama I am, just give me a challenge, and I will figure it out. Well, I got on the Internet and looked at all the recipes for French onion soup and then made up my own. I bought several types of beef broth to compare. Some canned brands were way too salty. Finally, through a taste test, I came up with the perfect soup. Cape was beside herself happy, and so, it was: mission accomplished!

3   large yellow onions (sliced thin)
1   stick unsalted butter
3   tablespoons olive oil
5   cups carton beef broth
3   cloves fresh garlic (minced)
2   teaspoons dried thyme
1   teaspoon Worcestershire sauce
Pinch of salt
Pinch of black pepper
French bread, sliced
Assorted grated cheeses (Gruyère,
    Swiss, Parmesan, Gouda, mozzarella)

1. In a stockpot, sauté onion with butter and olive oil. Add beef broth, garlic, thyme, Worcestershire sauce, salt, and pepper. Simmer for 30 minutes.
2. Preheat oven to broil.
3. Spoon soup into individual ovenproof serving bowls. Add 2 slices bread on top of each and top with the cheese assortment.
4. Broil until cheese has melted.

Cape and her dog, Bently, share a little moment on the porch.

SWEET POTATO PIE

———◆———

Put this pie on your buffet with real whipped cream on the side. Let everybody cut a slice and put a big scoop of whipped cream on top if they want it. This is a budget-friendly pie, so you can make two or three of them for the holidays.

1   stick salted butter (softened)
½   cup light brown sugar
½   cup granulated sugar
½   teaspoon ground nutmeg
½   teaspoon ground cinnamon
4   cups cooked sweet potato
        (about 3 large potatoes)
½   teaspoon vanilla extract
4   large eggs
½   cup whole milk
1   refrigerated piecrust
Whipped cream to serve

1. Preheat oven to 350°.
2. In a stand mixer, beat butter, brown sugar, granulated sugar, nutmeg, and cinnamon.
3. Peel the potatoes, cut them into cubes, and then boil them in water until tender. Drain in a colander. Add potato and vanilla to butter mixture. Mix well. Add in eggs, one at a time. Slowly add milk and mix.
4. Fit piecrust in a pie plate. Pour filling into piecrust. (This recipe makes a lot of filling. Use extra filling to make more pies or save to use later.)
5. Bake until filling is set and a knife comes out clean, about 55 minutes to 1 hour.

Cape, Bay, and Banks—silly sisters just enjoying each little moment

CORN CHOWDER

I serve this chowder with caramelized onions on top of each bowlful. That makes it pretty and adds a wonderful taste. The potatoes make the chowder really smooth. If it seems too thick, you can add more water or milk.

5   large russet potatoes (peeled and cut into cubes)
6½ cups water
7   tablespoons White Lily all-purpose flour
2   (14-ounce) cans cream-style corn
1   (14-ounce) can whole kernel corn (undrained)
2   cups whole milk
½   teaspoon salt
1   (8-ounce) package processed cheese product (cut into cubes)

1. In a stockpot, combine potatoes and 6 cups water. Bring to a boil over medium-high heat and cook until tender.
2. Combine flour and remaining ½ cup water, adding the water very slowly and stirring while pouring so no lumps will be present. Set aside.
3. Add all corn to potato mixture. Add milk and bring mixture to a slow boil. Pour in flour mixture very slowly while stirring. Add salt and processed cheese, stirring until combined.

KITCHEN WISDOM

You can find corn year-round in grocery stores, but you should get some fresh corn at farmers' markets and curbside stands during the summertime. That's when corn reaches its peak. You can tell it's fresh if the husk is green and you get a milky liquid when you prick the kernels with your fingernail.

chapter 6

TAILGATING

BAD INFLUENCE

I have no idea why folks throw empty cans and trash out onto the roadside, but they do. So many times, I have wanted to stop them and say, "What in the world are you doing? Didn't your mama teach you anything?" Once while I was picking up roadside trash, someone drove by and threw a can directly at me. I was shocked that anyone would do such a thing. Another time, when Dallas and Hannah were young, they joined me in picking up debris on Straughn School Road. There were several colorful beer cans in the trash pile. Children being children, Dallas and Hannah each picked out one of those colorful beer cans to play Kick the Can.

Later, we were all having the best time running, laughing, and kicking a beer can around the yard when George's parents drove up the drive. When Pawpaw saw what we were doing, he pitched a fit. You might as well say he told me off. He couldn't believe I let Dallas and Hannah play with those beer cans. "What would people say and think if they saw this?" Pawpaw asked. I thought, "What people? We live in the middle of the woods." I told him that the children weren't doing anything wrong, and neither was I. Well, his face turned red. He quickly turned his back to me, stomped back to his car with Granny inside, and backed down my narrow driveway only to hit a huge tree that knocked off his car's side mirror. Needless to say, he didn't visit us for weeks. I don't want to make out that Pawpaw was a bad man. He was a great man—a good leader, father, and husband. But sometimes, his temper got the best of him. I eventually threw the old beer cans away. I often remember that day and think you should live your life the best you can. There are always people who will try to find fault with everything. If you live your life trying to please others, you will be a miserable soul.

TASTY SNACK CRACKERS

———◆———

This indulgent treat tastes luxurious. They last well set out on a buffet or table for folks to nibble on with a cup of good black coffee.

1½ sleeves saltine crackers
2   sticks salted butter
2   cups light brown sugar
1   cup mini semisweet chocolate chips

1. Preheat oven to 400°. Line a rimmed baking sheet with heavy-duty foil. Grease the foil.
2. Place a single layer of crackers on the foil.
3. In a heavy-bottom saucepan, bring butter and brown sugar to a hard boil over medium-high heat. Let cook, stirring constantly, for 3½ minutes. (Do not let the sugar mixture stick to bottom of pan. Bubbles will form at this time.) Drizzle all the sugar mixture over the crackers. Lift each cracker with a butter knife so some of the mixture will go under the cracker to coat the other side.
4. Bake until crackers look a little brown and crunchy, about 8 minutes. Remove from oven and immediately sprinkle the chocolate chips on top of the crackers to melt. You can use the back of a spoon to spread the melted chocolate around on the crackers. Let cool completely.
5. Peel the crackers from the foil and break them apart. Store in an airtight container in the refrigerator.

CARAMEL POPCORN

—◆—

*Popcorn is very popular with my family. You can pop a cup
of popcorn kernels, and it will last you almost all afternoon. It's kind of
like those Sugar Daddy suckers of long ago. Mama would buy us a
Sugar Daddy, and we would see who could make theirs last the longest.
This recipe combines the best of both—popcorn and caramel.*

4   tablespoons vegetable oil
1⅓ cups popcorn kernels
1½ cups pecans
2   sticks unsalted butter
2   cups light brown sugar (firmly packed)
½   cup light corn syrup
½   teaspoon salt
½   teaspoon baking soda
½   teaspoon vanilla extract

1. Put the oil in a large pot with a lid, making sure you have enough to cover the bottom of the pan. Add popcorn and heat over medium heat, shaking the pan until a few kernels pop. Quickly cover with lid. Keep shaking the pan over the heat until no more kernels are popping. Remove from heat and place in a large bowl. Stir in pecans.

2. Preheat oven to 250°.

3. In a saucepan, melt butter, brown sugar, and corn syrup over medium heat. Cook for 5 minutes, stirring occasionally. Remove from heat and stir in salt, baking soda, and vanilla. Immediately, pour over popcorn and pecans, and stir with a wooden spoon. Spread popcorn mixture on a rimmed baking sheet.

4. Bake for 1 hour and 30 minutes, stirring every 15 minutes. Let cool. Store in an airtight container.

 *Life's Little Moments*

I didn't know about this little moment until the grandbabies became teenagers. That's when they confessed that when they were younger, after George and I were asleep in bed, they would sneak into the kitchen and eat ice cream and mayonnaise crackers. They told me all about it later and the fun they had being mischievous children.

SMOKED BOSTON BUTT

———◆———

I don't grill out often, but when I do, I love this Boston butt. Be sure to cover the pork with all the sugar and spice and then cook it low and slow for a real treat.

¼ cup smoked paprika
¼ cup light brown sugar (firmly packed)
3 tablespoons salt
2 tablespoons onion powder
2 tablespoons garlic powder
2 tablespoons dry mustard
2 tablespoons chili powder
2 tablespoons black pepper
2 teaspoons ground red pepper
1 (7- to 8-pound) bone-in Boston butt

1. Mix together paprika, brown sugar, salt, onion powder, garlic powder, dry mustard, chili powder, and peppers. Rub the mixture all over the pork. Wrap in plastic wrap; refrigerate for 12 to 24 hours.
2. Remove the pork from the refrigerator and let it set until it reaches room temperature, about 30 minutes.
3. Preheat your grill to 250°. Be sure to keep your heat low.
4. Remove plastic wrap and place pork on grill. Grill, covered, until a meat thermometer inserted in thickest portion registers 190°, about 7 hours and 30 minutes.
5. Remove from grill; wrap in foil. Let it sit for at least 30 minutes before shredding. You can use two forks or your hands. Eat it plain or make a sandwich. Either way, be sure to cover it completely with my Alabama White Sauce (recipe at right).

ALABAMA WHITE SAUCE

———◆———

All around Alabama, there are different versions of white barbecue sauce. I like the tangy taste of the vinegar with the smooth mayonnaise. Try this on your wings, grilled chicken, or pulled pork. Let it soak into the bread on any barbecue sandwich.

1½ cups mayonnaise
1 cup white vinegar
½ cup sugar
1 teaspoon ground white pepper
Juice of 1 lemon

1. In a jar, mix mayonnaise, vinegar, sugar, pepper, and lemon juice. Shake well until sugar is dissolved. Leftovers may be refrigerated for up to 1 week.

CORNMEAL MUFFINS

Oh, these are the best! Pile them high with pulled pork and douse it with Alabama White Sauce. You'll be back for seconds, I promise.

1½ cups White Lily buttermilk self-rising cornmeal
¼ cup sugar
2 large eggs
1 cup grated sharp Cheddar cheese
6 to 7 slices jarred jalapeño peppers (diced) or 1 fresh jalapeño pepper (diced)
1¼ cups whole buttermilk
Smoked Boston Butt (recipe on page 157)
Alabama White Sauce (recipe on page 157) to serve

1. Preheat oven to 400°. Grease a 12-cup muffin pan.
2. Combine cornmeal, sugar, eggs, cheese, and jalapeño, mixing well. Stir in buttermilk. Divide cornmeal mixture evenly into the wells of prepared pan.
3. Bake until lightly golden brown, about 20 minutes.
4. To make a slider: split your muffin in half, like a bun. Mound on your favorite Boston butt and spoon on Alabama White Sauce. Make sure you let plenty of sauce absorb into your muffin.

Life's Collections

The very best utensil to use for eating ice cream or a soft drink float is the iced tea spoon. This long-handled spoon can reach all the way down to the bottom of the float glass and scoop up all the goodie. None of mine have matching patterns! I'm fascinated by all the different designs. I have some that are real silver or silver-plated, and some are stainless steel. Doesn't matter—I love them all!

SWEET & SOUR MEATBALLS

A nice mix of sweet and savory, these meatballs are packed with flavor.
They are perfect for tailgating. You will be hard-pressed to eat just one!

Meatballs:
2   pounds ground beef
1   tablespoon salt
1   teaspoon ground red pepper
1   teaspoon oil

Sauce:
1   small onion (diced)
1   tablespoon salted butter
1   cup ketchup
1   cup water
1   cup light brown sugar
¼   cup apple cider vinegar
1   tablespoon dry mustard
1   tablespoon dried parsley
1   tablespoon paprika
1   teaspoon ground red pepper
1   teaspoon salt

1. For the meatballs: Mix together ground beef, salt, and red pepper. Form the meat mixture into balls about the size of a walnut. In a skillet, fry the meatballs in oil over medium heat turning so that all sides are browned. Remove from the pan and let drain.
2. For the sauce: In a skillet, sauté onion in butter. In a large saucepan over low heat, stir together ketchup and 1 cup water. Add onion mixture, brown sugar, vinegar, and all spices, and stir well.
3. Put meatballs in sauce. Stir gently, covering each meatball with sauce. Let cool and refrigerate overnight.
4. When ready to eat, simmer meatballs in the sauce until hot and bubbly. Serve with wooden picks.

Dallas and Hannah are decked out for the big game. Alabama Bambo! Roll Tide!

Banks, Cape, and Bay love their teams. Banks is wearing her Big Daddy's high school letterman sweater.

LUMPIA

If you make the Lumpia ahead of time, make sure to take them out of the refrigerator 30 minutes before cooking. This dish of Anna's is my favorite when I visit them.

1   (32-ounce) package spring roll wrappers
1½   pounds lean ground beef (can also use ground chicken or pork)
1   large potato (peeled and grated)
1   small container fresh mushrooms (grated)
2   large eggs (1 egg white separated and set aside)
3   green onions (finely chopped)
1   cup fresh bean sprouts (if available)
1 to 2 tablespoons soy sauce
½   teaspoon black pepper
Vegetable oil for frying
Sweet 'n' Sour Sauce (recipe at right)

1. Separate wrappers. Keep wrappers between two damp paper towels and cover with plastic wrap. (If wrappers dry out, they will break or crack.)
2. Mix all remaining ingredients except 1 egg white, oil, and sauce. Stir well.
3. To make lumpia, place 1 heaping tablespoon of beef mixture on 1 wrapper. Bring the bottom edge of the wrapper up and over the beef mixture. (They should be a little thicker than a thumb.) Then, fold over left and right edges of the wrapper and roll it towards the top edge. Use reserved egg white to seal the wrapper.
4. Heat oil in a skillet. When oil is hot, fry lumpia until golden brown. Drain on paper towels. Serve with Sweet 'n' Sour Sauce.

SWEET 'N' SOUR SAUCE

Serve Lumpia on a medium-size serving plate with a bowl of this sauce. Arrange the Lumpia on the plate all around the bowl. It is so good! Your family will enjoy this special, unusual treat.

6   tablespoons sugar
1   tablespoon cornstarch (heaping)
1   cup water
1   tablespoon ketchup
2   tablespoons white vinegar

1. In a small saucepan, mix sugar and cornstarch together. Slowly stir in 1 cup water until mixed well. Add ketchup and vinegar and stir until well combined. Cook over medium to medium-low heat, stirring continuously with a whisk, until mixture becomes translucent and comes to a slow boil.
2. Pour into a heatproof bowl and cover with a piece of plastic wrap directly on the surface. Let cool to room temperature to prevent a skin from forming.

SLOW COOKER MACARONI AND CHEESE

A classic recipe that makes everyone happy, you can put together this macaroni and cheese in a slow cooker, which also keeps it warm for tailgating. It's such a comforting dish!

1 (16-ounce) package elbow macaroni (cooked)
3½ cups whole milk
2½ cups grated sharp Cheddar cheese
1 pound cubed processed cheese product
1 (8-ounce) package cream cheese (cut into cubes and softened)
1 stick salted butter (melted)
½ teaspoon salt
½ cup chopped roasted red peppers

1. In 6-quart slow cooker, stir together cooked macaroni, milk, cheeses, butter, and salt. Cook on low for 6 to 8 hours, stirring every 2 hours. Just before serving, stir in red peppers.

My Tuscaloosa, Alabama, grandbabies, William and Isabella

Banks, Cape, and Hannah wear their team colors.

KITCHEN WISDOM

If the sauce gets too thick, add more milk, 1 tablespoon at a time, until you get the right consistency.

REDNECK NACHOS

There's no better dish to serve than nachos for a crowd pumped up to watch the big game. On game day, give your nachos a Southern twist with my Smoked Boston Butt (recipe on page 157) and Flo's Southern Barbecue Sauce below. Sit them on the coffee table as folks watch the game—they will gobble them up.

1   large bag kettle-cooked potato chips
2   pounds cooked Boston butt (pulled or chopped)
1   (1-ounce) envelope spicy ranch seasoning mix (prepared according to package instructions)
Flo's Southern Barbecue Sauce (recipe at right) or your favorite sweet barbecue sauce

1. On a large platter, empty the entire bag of chips.
2. Layer pork over the chips. Drizzle all over with ranch dressing and barbecue sauce. Serve immediately.

FLO'S SOUTHERN BARBECUE SAUCE

This is a good old-fashioned barbecue sauce you can slather on ribs, burgers, steaks, pork, and more! I like the mustard taste, but if you don't, just use less.

1   cup molasses
1   cup ketchup
1   cup white vinegar
1   cup yellow mustard
1   cup Worcestershire sauce
1   teaspoon ground red pepper

1. In a large saucepan, mix together molasses, ketchup, vinegar, mustard, Worcestershire sauce, and red pepper. Heat over medium heat and serve warm.

BROWNIES

I don't know a living soul who doesn't like brownies. Just give me milk in a metal cup and brownies on a saucer if you want me to stay happy. The first thing Walt goes for in my house is the buffet. He wants to see what there is to snack on. If brownies are there, he loads up.

1	stick salted butter
½	cup shortening
4	tablespoons cocoa powder
2	cups sugar
4	large eggs (room temperature)
1	cup White Lily all-purpose flour
2	teaspoons vanilla extract
1	cup pecans pieces

1. Preheat oven to 350°. Grease and flour a 13x9-inch baking dish.
2. In a saucepan, melt butter and shortening over low heat and let cool. Whisk in cocoa. Stir in sugar. Turn off burner and let mixture cool for at least 5 minutes. Add 1 egg at a time, stirring well after each. Whisk in flour. Add vanilla and pecans, stirring well. Pour into prepared pan.
3. Bake until a wooden pick inserted in the center comes out clean, about 30 minutes.

Hug us tight, Dallas!

A true fall celebration!

APPLE SPICE OATMEAL COOKIE SANDWICH

I am partial to a sandwich cookie, and these just have all the good flavors of fall with brown sugar, cinnamon, apple pie spice, and oatmeal. My Buttercream Icing makes the best-ever filling for these sweet delights.

1½ cups White Lily all-purpose flour
1   teaspoon baking powder
½   teaspoon apple pie spice
1   teaspoon ground cinnamon
1   teaspoon salt
2   sticks unsalted butter (softened)
1   cup light brown sugar
½   cup granulated sugar
2   large eggs
2   teaspoons vanilla extract
3   cups old-fashioned oats
½   cup chopped pecans
Buttercream Icing (recipe on
      page 249)

1. Preheat oven to 350°. Lightly grease a baking sheet.
2. Sift together flour, baking powder, apple pie spice, cinnamon, and salt in a medium bowl.
3. In a stand mixer, beat butter at medium speed until fluffy. Add sugars, beating well. Beat in eggs.
4. Add flour mixture to sugar mixture, and beat some more. Add vanilla and mix well. Fold in oats and pecans. Drop batter a tablespoonful at a time on baking sheet.
5. Bake until the cookies are soft and just set in center, 10 to 12 minutes. Let cool on pan.
6. When filling the cookies, the flat sides should face the inside. Fill with 2 tablespoons Buttercream Icing. Store in an airtight container in the refrigerator.

"A child's skinned knees will heal, but harsh and cruel words will forever leave deep scars."

chapter 7

HOLIDAY CLASSICS

THANKSGIVING DAY

I don't know if it's the falling leaves or the colors all through the yard and woods, but on Thanksgiving morning, when I'm wrapped up in my housecoat and sipping hot coffee on the front porch, the crispness of the cool, fresh air fills my spirit. I think of family. The grandchildren pop into my mind, and I instantly say a prayer for them. Dallas and Anna have such demanding jobs it's hard for them to make the long drive to join us. Walt and Hannah live just a skip and a hop away and will bring over special dishes in just a little while to celebrate Thanksgiving. I think of George and how we used to sit together on this porch. We had so many blessings on special Thanksgiving mornings. I miss him crumbling the cornbread for my dressing. Now, I do his job. Life has a way of moving forward.

I gather my thoughts, and after a while, everyone is here. We're telling old stories with lots of laughter, snapping pictures, and measuring the children's height on the closet door to see how much they have grown since last year. We still tell stories about Big Daddy (George), like the time he laid down in the inflatable plastic kiddie swimming pool in the front yard. What a sight to behold! The house is smelling so good with the turkey roasting in the oven and the dressing, too. It just wouldn't be Thanksgiving without a turkey, dressing, and cranberries.

The gorgeous 14-foot-long pine table sits right in the middle of our dining room. George made it just for me. I wanted it big enough so that the whole family could gather around, without having children at one table and adults at another. I've decorated it with fall leaves from the yard, berries, and pumpkins. Usually, the grandchildren make place cards for each of us. I don't know why they make them because we always sit in the very same place, but they do. It's probably because it's a tradition.

After we have eaten our fill, I cover all the leftovers with flour sacks that I have collected over the years. The colors and patterns remind me of old-time dresses. Folks used to make dresses, aprons, and curtains out of their flour sacks. I got this custom from my Granny, Bertha Hicks. It was always fun to go to her house and peek under the flour sack to see what food she had underneath. My mother never covered her leftovers with flour sacks. She used pot lids or put the food back in the oven until supper.

When suppertime rolls around, everybody is scattered, so each person just heats a plate of leftovers in the microwave. Some have gone hunting after lunch hoping to bring home a big buck for the freezer. Some have gone for a walk in the woods, and some have played "beauty shop," as Banks calls it. That's when we fix each other's makeup, braid hair, or massage feet. Late in the afternoon, Hannah, Anna, and I like to fix a pot of coffee and have a piece of pie or cake.

Thanksgiving is a relaxing time for me—no presents to buy and cooler weather after a long, hot Alabama summer. It's a time for wearing cozy sweaters and enjoying hot chocolate, boiled peanuts, ball games, bonfires, and orange pumpkins everywhere. A feeling of thankfulness fills my heart with gladness, and I get a new lease on life as I count my blessings. I want to celebrate. I hope you, too, remember your blessings at Thanksgiving and where your blessings came from. Thank you, Lord!

"*You can't change your children, your mate, your friend, or anybody, but you can love, cherish, and pray for them.*"

ORANGE BUTTERMILK SALAD

Old-fashioned gelatin salad never goes out of style as a colorful side dish to dress up any buffet.

1   (20-ounce) can crushed pineapple (drained)
3   tablespoons sugar
1   (6-ounce) box orange gelatin
2   cups whole buttermilk
1   (8-ounce) container frozen whipped topping (thawed)
1   cup chopped pecans

1. In a boiler, combine pineapple and sugar and bring to a boil over medium-high heat. When the pineapple mixture begins to boil, immediately add gelatin and stir until dissolved. Remove from heat and allow to cool down a bit.
2. Stir in buttermilk and place in refrigerator until partially set.
3. Fold in whipped topping and pecans. Pour into an oiled mold or just pour into a pretty serving bowl. Refrigerate overnight.

Walt and Hannah celebrate the New Year, and William joins in.

YE ARE THE SALT OF THE EARTH: BUT IF THE SALT HAVE LOST HIS SAVOUR, WHEREWITH SHALL IT BE SALTED? IT IS THENCEFORTH GOOD FOR NOTHING, BUT TO BE CAST OUT, AND TO BE TRODDEN UNDER FOOT OF MEN.
—MATTHEW 5:13, KJV

BEEF TENDERLOIN

This is the most tender roast you'll ever eat, but remember to follow the directions and keep the oven door closed for eight minutes. It's a good dish to serve to company or at holidays with mushrooms and bacon-wrapped green beans on the side.

1 (3-pound) beef tenderloin
¼ cup stone-ground mustard
Steak seasoning of your choice (I like mine heavy on garlic)
½ cup apple juice or cider
½ stick salted butter

1. Rinse the tenderloin and pat dry. Rub the entire tenderloin with mustard and steak seasoning. Pour apple juice into a large resealable plastic bag and then put the tenderloin inside and seal. Refrigerate overnight to marinate.
2. Remove tenderloin from refrigerator and discard the marinade. Let tenderloin come to room temperature before cooking.
3. Preheat oven to 425°.
4. In a black cast-iron skillet, heat butter over medium-high heat. When butter is hot, place tenderloin in skillet and sear for 2 to 3 minutes. Turn tenderloin and sear the other side for 2 to 3 minutes. Immediately place tenderloin in a roasting pan with a rack. Pour remaining butter in skillet over tenderloin.
5. Bake for 18 to 22 minutes and turn the oven off. Do not open the oven door. Allow to sit in oven for 8 minutes. Remove from oven and let stand for 10 minutes.

SAUTÉED MUSHROOMS

Sometimes, I think we only get sautéed mushrooms when we go out to eat. You can easily do these at home. Get busy and make some. My Isabella likes mushrooms any way I fix them—stuffed, sautéed, or fried.

1 stick salted butter
1 (16-ounce) package sliced fresh mushrooms
1 tablespoon Worcestershire sauce
½ teaspoon garlic salt

1. In a skillet, melt butter over medium heat. Add mushrooms, Worcestershire sauce, and garlic salt. Reduce heat to medium-low and cook until mushrooms are tender and almost all liquid is gone, about 20 to 25 minutes.

SWEET POTATO CAKE

Who would have ever thought of making a cake with sweet potatoes? Well, here it is! It ranks as one of the best. It's so moist and scrumptious that you will find yourself cutting another piece to go with that second cup of coffee. If you make it once, you will make it again and again.

2   cups sugar
2   sticks salted butter
3   large eggs (room temperature)
1   tablespoon vanilla extract
2½   cups cooked mashed sweet potatoes
2½   cups White Lily all-purpose flour
2   teaspoons baking soda
2   teaspoons baking powder
1   tablespoon ground cinnamon
1   tablespoon ground ginger
1   teaspoon ground nutmeg
½   teaspoon salt
1   cup whole buttermilk (room temperature)
1   cup pecans (large pieces)
Spiced Cream Cheese Icing (recipe on page 245)

1. Preheat oven to 350°. Grease and flour 2 (9-inch) cake pans and line bottom of each with parchment paper.
2. In a stand mixer, beat sugar and butter until very creamy, 5 minutes. Add eggs, one at a time, beating after each addition. Beat in vanilla and sweet potatoes.
3. In a separate bowl, mix flour, baking soda, baking powder, cinnamon, ginger, nutmeg, and salt. Stir together well.
4. Add the flour mixture to the sugar mixture in mixer, alternating with the buttermilk and beating until combined. Fold pecans into the batter.
5. Divide the batter into the pans.
6. Bake for 35 to 40 minutes or until a wooden pick inserted in the center comes out clean. Let cake sit for 10 to 15 minutes before removing from pan. Let cake cool completely, then halve each to make 4 layers. Ice with Spiced Cream Cheese Icing.

"Driving slowly, praying, thinking, and reminiscing will change your outlook on life."

CINNAMON PICKLES

These bright red pickles are like candy. Make a batch of them for gifts and to keep on hand for unexpected visitors. They are so crispy!

7   pounds large cucumbers
1   cup pickling lime
3   cups white vinegar
4   tablespoons red food coloring
1   tablespoon alum
2   cups water
7   cups sugar
7   cinnamon sticks
12   ounces red mini cinnamon-flavored candies (like Red Hots)

1. Peel and seed cucumbers and cut into strips or rings. In a glass bowl (do not use plastic or metal), mix pickling lime, cucumbers, and enough water to cover cucumbers, and let sit for 24 hours. Drain and rinse several times to remove all traces of lime. You must be sure to rinse them completely.

2. Soak cucumbers in ice water for 3 hours. Drain. In a large pot, mix 1 cup vinegar, food coloring, alum, cucumbers, and enough water to cover, and simmer for 2 hours. Drain. Return cucumbers to pot.

3. In a medium saucepan, boil remaining 2 cups vinegar, 2 cups water, sugar, cinnamon sticks, and candies, then simmer until all is dissolved. Pour over cucumbers and let sit for 24 hours. Bring to boil again and pack into hot jars.

KITCHEN WISDOM

I put the flat lids into a pot of water, bring it to a boil, then turn down the heat to a simmer to keep them really hot as I am filling jars. I have found that it helps my jars to seal if I put the flat lids on the jars while the flats are hot.

CORN CASSEROLE

*Corn is a staple on any Southern table, but this casserole gussies it up a bit
with oodles of bacon, a little sweetness, and cheesy goodness.
The whole family adores this one.*

1   pound sliced bacon
½   onion (chopped)
1   clove garlic (minced)
⅔   cup White Lily self-rising flour
⅔   cup White Lily self-rising cornmeal
¼   cup sugar
1   cup sour cream
1   stick salted butter (melted)
1   (15-ounce) can whole kernel corn
     (drained)
1   (15-ounce) can cream-style corn
2   large eggs
1½   cups grated sharp Cheddar cheese
3   green onions (chopped)

1. Preheat oven to 375°. Grease a
baking dish.
2. In a skillet, fry bacon. Let it drain on
a paper towel and crumble. Save bacon
grease. Sauté chopped onion and garlic
in a spoonful of the bacon drippings.
3. In a large bowl, combine flour, cornmeal,
and sugar. In a separate bowl, mix sour
cream, butter, all corn, and eggs. Stir well.
4. Add onion mixture and half of the
bacon to corn mixture. Stir well. Add
corn mixture to flour mixture. Stir
well. Pour into prepared baking dish.
5. Bake for 35 minutes. Remove casserole
from oven and top with cheese and
remaining bacon. Bake until cheese is
completely melted. Top with green onion.

Life's Collections

When I was a little girl, I would take scissors and
cut out paper dolls from our Sears, Roebuck and
Company catalogs. I cut out a daddy, a mama,
children, and furniture. I found outfits for each
one. On Sunday afternoons, one of my very favorite
things to do was to play and pretend with my
homemade paper dolls. Now, I just collect paper
dolls and remember the good times I had.

WARM GOAT CHEESE SPREAD

Soft goat cheese and fig preserves make for a yummy appetizer to spread on crusty French bread rounds. You'll be the talk of the party if you bring this delicious dish.

1 (12-ounce) loaf crusty French bread
½ stick salted butter (softened)
1 (8-ounce) log plain goat cheese
¾ cup fig jam or preserves (about half a jar)
¼ cup pistachios (chopped)

1. Preheat oven to 350°.
2. Slice your French bread into thin appetizer slices but leave together in a loaf. Butter between each slice and wrap the loaf tightly in foil.
3. Bake for 30 to 40 minutes. Open foil and bake a little longer. (You want the bread to be crispy.)
4. Slice goat cheese log straight down the middle lengthwise, so you have 2 long pieces. Put end to end in a medium baking dish or an ovenproof platter and cover with fig jam.
5. Bake, uncovered, until soft and bubbly, about 10 to 12 minutes.
6. Sprinkle pistachios on top of cheese and serve with bread.

Cape and William enjoy a beautiful day in rocking chairs.

Isabella makes a turkey with a pine cone and real feathers that Big Daddy found.

AND WE KNOW THAT ALL THINGS WORK TOGETHER FOR GOOD TO THEM THAT LOVE GOD, TO THEM WHO ARE CALLED ACCORDING TO HIS PURPOSE. —ROMANS 8:28, KJV

GREEN BEAN BUNDLES

These fancy green beans take some time to fix, but they will make your guests feel so special. It's worth taking this extra step, especially on holidays, to create a wonderful memory for family and friends.

4   cans whole green beans, drained
1   pound sliced bacon (cut in thirds crosswise)
1   cup brown sugar
½   stick salted butter (melted)

1. Preheat oven to 375°. Grease a rimmed baking sheet.
2. Create bundles by stacking 4 or 5 beans together. Wrap each stack with 1 bacon strip. Place bundles on the prepared baking sheet.
3. Mix brown sugar and melted butter. Sprinkle on top of the beans. Bake until beans are tender and bacon looks brown and crunchy, about 35 to 45 minutes.

"The Fall Olympics." We had a shooting contest, and the winners stood at different heights like at the Olympic Games. First place in the shooting contest was Anna; second place was George, and third place was Mary Ann, George's sister.

Banks celebrates the New Year.

PINEAPPLE CASSEROLE

This is a dish you'll find on Southern tables, especially at holiday time. You can cut back a little on the sugar if you don't want it too sweet. It's the grandbabies' favorite.

2 (15.5-ounce) cans pineapple chunks (drained and juice reserved)
6 tablespoons reserved pineapple juice
1 large egg (lightly beaten)
1 cup sugar
6 tablespoons While Lily all-purpose flour
2 cups grated sharp Cheddar cheese
1 stick salted butter
1 sleeve round buttery crackers (crushed)

1. Preheat oven to 250°. Grease a casserole dish.
2. Place pineapple chunks in the casserole dish.
3. In a boiler, combine reserved 6 tablespoons pineapple juice, egg, sugar, and flour. Cook over low heat until slightly thickened. Add cheese and stir. Remove from heat and pour over pineapple chunks in the dish.
4. Melt butter and mix with crushed crackers. Spread cracker mixture over the top of casserole.
5. Bake until bubbly, 30 to 35 minutes.

Life's Little Moments

On cold winter mornings before the sun came up, our alarm clock would ring out into the darkness. Time to get up for work! George would stay in bed under a ton of homemade quilts. I'd stumble to the kitchen to put on the coffee and then hurry back and crawl in bed beside him. The bedroom was chilly and dark, but his body warmed me as we'd snuggle up close beside each other. Not saying a word nor moving, George and I just enjoyed the little moments of snuggling together on cold mornings while we waited for the smell of fresh coffee to get us moving for the day.

TENNESSEE JAM CAKE

"If I had known you were coming, I would have baked you a cake."
Have y'all ever heard that old saying before? You can bake this cake for
company. One of my social media followers from Tennessee sent me
a jam cake recipe, and I switched it up to my liking—y'all know I'm bad about
doing that. Anyway, put this cake on your buffet, and your family may
just clean the plate for you.

Cake:
2   sticks salted butter (softened)
1½   cups granulated sugar
4   large eggs
10   ounces strawberry or raspberry preserves
2½   cups White Lily all-purpose flour
1   teaspoon baking soda
1   teaspoon ground nutmeg
1   teaspoon ground cinnamon
1   teaspoon ground cloves
¼   teaspoon salt
1   cup whole buttermilk
1½   cups chopped pecans

Icing:
2   sticks salted butter
2   cups light brown sugar (firmly packed)
¼   cup plus 2 tablespoons whole milk
3   cups powdered sugar

1. Preheat oven to 350°. Grease and flour 3 (9-inch) cake pans. Cut 3 circles of parchment paper and line the bottom of each pan with paper.
2. For the cake: In a stand mixer, beat butter and granulated sugar until fluffy. Add eggs, one at a time, and mix well. Add preserves and mix.

3. In a large bowl, stir together flour, baking soda, nutmeg, cinnamon, cloves, and salt. Gradually add the flour mixture to the butter mixture, alternately with buttermilk, and mix well. Fold in the pecans. Pour the batter evenly into prepared cake pans.
4. Bake for 35 minutes. Let cool.
5. For the icing: In a saucepan, heat butter, brown sugar, and milk. Bring to a boil. Remove from heat and let cool for at least 10 minutes.
6. In a stand mixer, beat powdered sugar and cooled butter mixture.
7. Spread the icing between each cake layer. (You may need to add milk, 1 teaspoon at a time, if the icing is too stiff and hard to smooth out on the cake layers.) Then, spread icing on the sides and top. After the cake has been iced, put some extra powdered sugar in a sifter and sprinkle a little on top of the cake.

chapter 8

COOKIE SWAP

SWEETGUM BOTTOM ANTIQUES

There was an 1875 farmhouse that sat vacant just off Highway 29 North in Andalusia, Alabama. Every time George and I went to town, I would look at that old, stately house, and in my heart, I always wanted it. Early one morning, we were headed to town, and I spied a "for sale" sign right in the front yard of the house. I could hardly sit in my seat I was so excited. I said, "Oh, George! I want that house!" Well, being the generous soul he was, George replied, "I'll see what I can do to buy it for you." He was always ready to spend money on what I really wanted. But, he actually loved that old house, too. We didn't know at the time what we were going to do with another house, but it seemed to be calling our names. I knew the old house had many memories to share, if it could just talk. It had no paint left on it after many years of neglect, and its tin roof was rusted and aged. A plain light bulb next to the front door was always on night and day. When passing by, I often wondered why the owner didn't just turn the electricity off. Well, we bought the old house a few days later at the amazing price of only $1,000. The catch? We would have to move the house if we wanted it. The land was not for sale. We cleared off a spot next to our house and hired a house mover for $2,500 to get it to our property. Mind you, we still didn't know how we would use the house.

Hannah was in seventh grade—the age when all girls get embarrassed easily and think everybody sees every pimple on their face. She was embarrassed about this old house. She expressed her feelings, too. "Mama, this is the ugliest house. It's messing up our property," Hannah said. She told me that, when she grew up, she'd have a modern house in town with sidewalks and chrome and glass furniture. I couldn't help but laugh. She's grown now with three girls of her own. Wouldn't you know it, she and her husband, Walt, and their girls live surrounded with antiques in a solid wood house with a tin roof smack in the middle of the woods—a far cry from town. Guess she grew out of that embarrassing teenage time because she now loves old, unusual things and the sound of the rain on their tin roof.

George and I worked tirelessly on the house—cleaning, painting the inside, putting in a center hallway entrance. We finally decided to turn it into a shop that we named Sweetgum Bottom Antiques. We had a grand opening, and customers poured in every weekend. Business was wonderful. One afternoon, an elderly lady came by to look through what we had to offer. We sat together in rocking chairs on the front porch. She knew the history of the house because she had lived there as a girl. I wrote down every word she had to say about the old house. The original owners had a grown son who ran away one night. His mama told her family to just leave that porch light on for him. She was hoping he'd come back and see the light on and maybe he'd know all was well. But, her boy never came home. He ran away and stayed away. I made a promise in my heart that I would try to leave that light on by the front door as long as I could in memory of her son. For years and years, George and I would always replace that light bulb. When my George passed away in 2018, I closed the shop and turned off all the lights because I knew my soulmate would never return. My George had gone to his heavenly home, and one day, I, too, will follow the light of the world—Jesus—to meet them both in Heaven.

The old house still stands today on our property. We added tons of memories to every room. I'm sure of that. Our grandchildren played under its porches, tried on ladies' hats, played school at the old desk, peddled the old pump organ, and made mud cakes to sell. They read comic books, raced toy cars, and had tea parties. Isabella, William, Bay, Cape, and Banks could probably write a book about that old house. George and I never regretted buying and moving that old house with all its old smells, its squeaky floors, and the pitter-patter of our grandbabies' tiny feet running among all the treasures. Sometimes, our hearts lead, and we must follow. I'm glad we did.

BELLAIRE LOG COOKIES

These cookies make great Christmas gifts. Wrap each cookie dough log in wax paper, freeze, and tie a pretty red ribbon on each end of the log. Include the instructions so folks can bake these cookies right away or put them in the freezer for baking later.

2	sticks salted butter (softened)
2	cups sugar
2	large eggs
2	cups White Lily all-purpose flour
1	teaspoon baking soda
2	pinches of salt
1	teaspoon ground nutmeg
1	teaspoon ground cinnamon
1¼	cups chopped pecans
1	cup sweetened flaked coconut
1	cup raisins

1. Using a stand mixer, beat butter and sugar until light and smooth. Add eggs and mix well.

2. In a separate bowl, stir flour, baking soda, salt, nutmeg, and cinnamon. Add flour mixture to the butter mixture, beating until combined. Add pecans, coconut, and raisins and stir well.

3. With floured hands, divide dough and roll into 4 (5-inch-long) logs 2 inches in diameter. Wrap each log in wax paper. Refrigerate overnight or freeze until ready to bake.

4. Preheat oven to 400°.

5. Slice logs into ½-inch-thick pieces and place on a baking sheet.

6. Bake until golden brown, about 10 to 12 minutes.

William tries his hand in the kitchen.

" If you are ninety and your child is seventy, your concern for them remains. It will never end."

DAINTY ROSEMARY COOKIES

The wonderful herb flavor of these pretty cookies makes them taste even better than they look. You have to chop the rosemary very small so its flavor isn't too strong. Mince it once and then do it again!

1   cup White Lily all-purpose flour
1   stick unsalted butter (softened)
½   cup powdered sugar
2   tablespoons fresh rosemary leaves (minced very, very small)
2   teaspoons granulated sugar
1   teaspoon fresh lemon juice

1. Preheat oven to 350°. Lightly grease a baking sheet.
2. In a stand mixer, combine all the ingredients and mix until the dough sticks together.
3. Roll dough into 1-inch balls and place on prepared baking sheet. Press each ball down with the bottom of a glass. (If the dough is sticking, lightly coat the bottom of the the glass with flour.)
4. Bake until light brown around the edges, about 10 minutes. Let cool a few minutes on the pan before removing.

Life's Little Moments

To go anywhere in our house, you must first go through the kitchen. It's in the middle of our home. Bay, Isabella, Cape, and Banks stop to sneak a pinch of raw biscuit dough. William passes through to grab another cookie. Dallas always does a taste test from my pot on the stove. Walt searches for a piece of chocolate. Anna helps me cook, and Hannah fills up iced tea glasses with ice. All of this happening right there in the kitchen makes me realize our blessings. When George was with us, he would sit at the kitchen table and talk with any of us who would sit down with him awhile. Sweet little moments are still happening here in the kitchen. We're blessed.

"OH, SO CRISPY" COOKIES

If I leave a plate of these in the kitchen, they'll disappear. The little bit of nutmeg gives the cookies just a touch of spiciness. And, they are just as their name says—crispy in texture.

1	stick salted butter (softened)
½	cup granulated sugar
½	cup light brown sugar
1	large egg
1	teaspoon vanilla extract
1	cup White Lily all-purpose flour (sifted)
1	teaspoon baking powder
1	teaspoon baking soda
½	teaspoon salt
¼	teaspoon ground nutmeg
1	cup old-fashioned rolled oats
1	cup sweetened flaked coconut

1. Preheat oven to 350°.
2. In a stand mixer, beat butter until creamy. Gradually add sugars, beating well after each addition. Add egg and vanilla. Beat until light and fluffy.
3. Sift together flour, baking powder, baking soda, salt, and nutmeg. Add flour mixture to sugar mixture, beating well. Stir in oats and coconut.
4. Drop batter by tablespoonfuls onto a baking sheet.
5. Bake for 10 to 12 minutes.

I painted the words on this old saw blade. It was George's granddaddy's saw blade for logging.

George and I collected bottles and kept them in our barn.

CAN'T-BE-BEAT COOKIES

The name of the recipe says it all. This makes a thick batter that gives you a rich, delicious cookie.

1 (15.25-ounce) box chocolate cake mix
½ stick salted butter (melted)
1 (8-ounce) package cream cheese (softened and cut into small cubes)
3 large eggs
3 cups powdered sugar
½ cup White Lily all-purpose flour
1 cup pecans (chopped)

1. Preheat oven to 350°. Lightly grease a baking sheet.
2. In a stand mixer, beat cake mix, melted butter, cream cheese, and 1 egg until everything is mixed and moist. Add the remaining 2 eggs and mix. Add in powdered sugar and mix. Add flour and mix. Stir in pecans.
3. Drop the batter by teaspoonfuls on prepared pan.
4. Bake for 12 to 14 minutes. Allow cookies to cool on the pan a few minutes before you remove them.

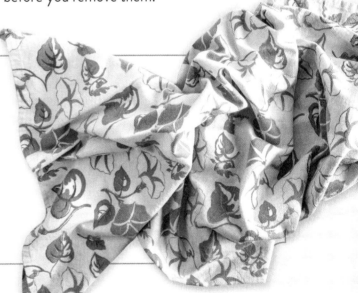

I SAY UNTO YOU, THAT LIKEWISE JOY SHALL BE IN HEAVEN OVER ONE SINNER THAT REPENTETH, MORE THAN OVER NINETY AND NINE JUST PERSONS, WHICH NEED NO REPENTANCE.
—LUKE 15:7, KJV

KITCHEN WISDOM

You might want to use two flatware teaspoons—one to scoop the batter and the other to push it onto the cookie sheet.

WEDDING COOKIES

Bring a tin of these delicate, light cookies to a special bride in your life, or make them for her wedding day. Be sure to save some for you to have as a snack with a cup of coffee.

2 sticks salted butter (softened)
½ cup powdered sugar (plus more for coating)
1 teaspoon vanilla extract
¾ cup pecans (chopped very small)
2¼ cups White Lily all-purpose flour (sifted)
¼ teaspoon salt

1. Preheat oven to 400°.
2. In a stand mixer, beat butter and powdered sugar until light and fluffy. Stir in vanilla and pecans.
3. Whisk together flour and salt. Add flour mixture to butter mixture and mix well. Chill dough for 15 minutes.
4. Form dough into 1¼-inch balls. Place balls on an ungreased baking sheet lined with parchment paper.
5. Bake until light brown, 10 to 12 minutes. Let cool completely. Roll in powdered sugar until coated.

Anna and Dallas got married in 2002 at Hickory Ridge Lodge.

Hannah and Walt got married in 1998 at The Cottle House Bed & Breakfast.

CRUNCHY TOASTED COOKIES

Old-fashioned oats and sweet coconut are mixed together and toasted to make these cookies. They are so good that they will never make it to the cookie jar.

2   cups old-fashioned oats
1   cup sweetened flaked coconut
2   sticks salted butter
1   cup granulated sugar (plus more for topping)
½   cup light brown sugar (firmly packed)
2   large eggs
2   teaspoons vanilla extract
1½ cups White Lily all-purpose flour
½   teaspoon salt
½   teaspoon baking soda
½   teaspoon ground cinnamon

1. Preheat oven to 350°. Grease a baking sheet with butter.
2. Spread oats and coconut into bottom of a large casserole dish. Bake, stirring every 5 minutes until tender and toasted, about 20 minutes. Increase the oven temperature to 375°.
3. In a stand mixer, beat butter, sugars, eggs, and vanilla together until light and fluffy.
4. In a bowl, stir flour, salt, baking soda, cinnamon, toasted oats, and toasted coconut. Add the flour mixture to the sugar mixture, beating until combined.
5. Using floured hands, roll batter into small balls and place on prepared baking sheet. (They will spread out very flat, so don't put them close to each other.)
6. Get out a small bowl and add a little granulated sugar. Dip the bottom of a glass in the sugar to coat it. Then, press down very lightly on each cookie ball. (The more sugar you get on the bottom of the glass, the less sticky it will be at this job.)
7. Bake for 8 or 9 minutes. The shape of the cookies should be large and paper-thin when they are ready. Let cool on the pan a few minutes and then slide a spatula under to remove from pan.

Bay gets a taste of some Hershey's chocolate syrup.

COOKIE CAKE

—◆—

Slather my Buttercream Icing over this cake, and you can use it for special occasions, especially for children who might prefer cookies to cake.

2   sticks salted butter (softened)
¾   cup granulated sugar
¾   cup light brown sugar
2   large eggs
1   teaspoon vanilla extract
2¼   cups White Lily all-purpose flour
1   teaspoon baking soda
1   teaspoon salt
1   (12-ounce) bag semisweet chocolate chips
Buttercream Icing (recipe on page 249)

1. Preheat oven to 350°. Use butter wrappers to grease a rimmed 13x9-inch baking sheet.
2. In a stand mixer, beat butter, granulated sugar, and brown sugar. Add eggs, one at a time, to sugar mixture, beating well. Add vanilla.
3. In a bowl, stir together flour, baking soda, and salt. Gradually add flour mixture to sugar mixture, beating until combined. Stir in chocolate chips. Press batter into prepared baking sheet.
4. Bake for 15 to 20 minutes. Let cool completely before decorating with my Buttercream Icing.

Sharing a moment of worship together at Bethany Baptist Church

"Being happy with yourself makes others happy to be near you."

Sage

KITCHEN WISDOM

I usually double this recipe and make it in a three-quarter sheet pan. Don't worry. There won't be any leftovers!

LACE COOKIES

—————◆—————

Watch these cookies carefully while they bake because they can easily burn.

2   cups old-fashioned oats
2   tablespoons White Lily all-purpose flour
1½ cups sugar
2   teaspoons baking powder
½   teaspoon salt
2   sticks salted butter (melted)
2   large eggs (beaten)
3   teaspoons vanilla extract
2½ cups pecans (chopped)

1. In a large bowl, stir oats, flour, sugar, baking powder, and salt. Pour hot melted butter over the oats mixture, stirring until sugar dissolves.
2. Beat eggs and vanilla until blended.

Add egg mixture and pecans to oats mixture. Stir well. Let the batter sit for 30 minutes before preheating the oven. (This step is very important!)
3. Preheat oven to 325°. Line a baking sheet with aluminum foil.
4. Drop level teaspoonfuls of batter onto the foil about 2 inches apart. (If you put too much batter on the foil, the cookies will run together.)
5. Bake for 10 to 13 minutes. (Watch carefully because the cookies will burn easily.) Remove foil with cookies from the pan. Let cool and then peel cookies from foil. You can reuse the foil for more batches.

Life's Collections

I rarely use a cookie cutter. The only time I use them is at Christmastime. The ones with wooden handles that are painted green, red, and yellow are my favorite. I've never seen a cookie cutter with a wooden handle that was any other color. There's just something about those old painted wooden handles that make me want to make Christmas ornaments in the shape of cookies to hang on our Christmas tree.

CHOCOLATE COOKIE BALLS

In this very useful recipe, you can substitute cookie flavors and coatings to mix and match whatever your taste buds enjoy. The round shape makes them stand out so pretty on a platter!

1 (20-ounce) package cream-filled chocolate sandwich cookies (not double-stuffed)
1 (8-ounce) package cream cheese (room temperature and cubed)
1 (24-ounce) package vanilla almond bark or white candy coating

1. Place cookies in a resealable plastic bag and crush them using a rolling pin.
2. In the food processor, add cream cheese to the cookie crumbs and pulse until a dough ball forms. Or, place cookie crumbs in a bowl and mix in the cream cheese with clean hands until dough comes together. Chill dough in refrigerator for at least 1 hour.
3. Form dough balls about 1 inch in diameter. Set on a baking sheet and place back in refrigerator.
4. Melt almond bark or candy coating according to package directions. Using two forks, dip cookie balls into coating mixture and cover completely, tapping excess coating off. Place the coated cookie ball on a baking sheet lined with parchment or wax paper.

> I AM ALPHA AND OMEGA, THE BEGINNING AND THE ENDING, SAITH THE LORD, WHICH IS, AND WHICH WAS, AND WHICH IS TO COME, THE ALMIGHTY. —REVELATION 1:8, KJV

KITCHEN WISDOM

You can use vanilla or chocolate cookies with butterscotch coating. You can also use peanut butter cookies with chocolate coating, cream-filled vanilla sandwich cookies with chocolate coating, or cream-filled lemon sandwich cookies with vanilla coating. Be creative and try them all!

chapter 9

WARM BREADS

DANCING IN THE KITCHEN

One of my very favorite memories of my George is of us dancing in the kitchen. We had danced in the kitchen many times. Sometimes, it was me making the first move; sometimes, it was him. But, one particular dance on a cold winter day is very special to my heart. The sink was full of dirty dishes, and flour covered me and the children, too. We had been frying chicken for supper—one of George's favorite meals. Everything was a big mess. I was on the verge of throwing up my hands and letting out a big scream like a peacock in the farmyard. George eased over to me. He gently slid his arms around my waist while I was standing at the sink with my apron on and holding a wet dishrag in my hand. He gently turned me around. I dropped that old rag in the soapy water and turned to him. He held me tightly as an old favorite love song of ours played on a black plastic radio. My heart melted. That kitchen mess left my mind as I focused on him and his love for me. He kissed my neck, and we slowly danced around the kitchen. The good Lord surely knew what He was doing when He created the blessing of marriage. We were created to love God and to love each other. As the song ended, George and I hugged each other tight, and I got back to the sink of dirty dishes while George returned to helping the kids with their homework. I feel thankful that God provided time for us to enjoy each other's embrace. What a wonderful moment together we had dancing in the kitchen. George has gone to Heaven now, but often, when it's winter and cold outside and I am elbow-deep in warm soapy dishwater, I think of him and his embrace. Life is good, y'all. Open your heart and your eyes; you'll see what even the small blessings can do for your spirit. Life is way too short not to enjoy the little moments like dancing in the kitchen.

BUTTERMILK CORNBREAD

Cornbread is such a staple on Southern tables that everybody has two or three recipes for a little variety. If you are new to making cornbread, you will want to start with this buttermilk version. It is the simplest recipe I have and goes well with any meal.

3 tablespoons vegetable oil
1¾ cups White Lily self-rising buttermilk cornmeal
1½ cups whole buttermilk
¼ cup sugar
1 large egg

1. Preheat oven to 450°.
2. In an 8-inch cast-iron skillet, heat the vegetable oil over medium-high heat. (Your oil should be moving around and dancing in the skillet before you pour in your cornbread mixture.)
3. In a bowl, combine cornmeal, buttermilk, sugar, and egg. With a rubber spatula, mix well until batter is blended. Once the oil is hot, pour batter into skillet. (It should sizzle.) Immediately put the skillet into the oven.
4. Bake until lightly golden brown, about 22 to 25 minutes. Turn cornbread out onto a plate to serve.

"When stressed and bewildered with a situation, realize that there is a higher power at work in your life."

Life's Little Moments

The grandchildren are coming up the driveway. Excitement fills your heart. When they open the car door, you rush out to meet them with a huge smile on your face and open arms. Y'all, hug and kiss with never-ending love. These little moments are the best moments of all!

ORANGE-PECAN
SLICE BREAD

This bread is so pretty with the pieces of orange candy in it. You can give it to your friends as a gift for any holiday, from Easter to Christmas.

3   cups White Lily all-purpose flour
4   teaspoons baking powder
½   teaspoon salt
½   cup sugar
3   tablespoons salted butter (melted)
1   large egg
¾   cup whole milk
1   teaspoon orange zest
¼   cup fresh orange juice
½   teaspoon vanilla extract
⅓   cup chopped pecans
⅓   cup chopped orange slice candy

1. Preheat oven to 350°. Grease a 8x4-inch loaf pan and sprinkle in a little flour.
2. In a medium bowl, stir together flour, baking powder, salt, and sugar.
3. In a large bowl, whisk together butter, egg, milk, orange zest and juice, and vanilla.
4. Fold butter mixture into flour mixture until moistened. Stir in pecans and orange candy.
5. Bake for about 1 hour, shielding with foil if needed to avoid overbrowning.

Banks and William work on an art project.

Big Daddy and Cape play in the leaves.

SOUR CREAM CORNBREAD

Cornbread is so versatile. I make it all different ways. I like serving this recipe with just about anything.

1   (8.5-ounce) box cornbread mix
3   large eggs (beaten)
1   cup sour cream
½   cup olive oil
½   (14.75-ounce) can cream-style corn
½   cup sugar
Pinch of salt

1. Preheat oven to 350°. Grease an 11x7-inch casserole dish.
2. Combine cornbread mix, eggs, sour cream, olive oil, corn, sugar, and salt. Stir well. Pour into prepared dish.
3. Bake until golden brown, about 40 minutes.

Isabella and Anna share mama and daughter time.

Life's Collections

George and I just couldn't turn down an old rolling pin in an antiques store. For me, I guess it brought back the memory of my precious Mama making delicious dumplings. Each rolling pin was held by the hands of some sweet soul cooking for their family. In our collection, some are new, some are handmade, and all are special to me. I will never know who held each one, but I know for sure they were held by someone who cared.

BROCCOLI CORNBREAD

Church functions mean food! I don't think I've ever been to a Bethany Baptist Church function where I didn't see a big casserole dish of Broccoli Cornbread. The broccoli adds delicious flavor and a festive color to cornbread. Heck, if you put some meat in it, it would be a complete meal!

2   (8.5-ounce) packages cornbread mix
4   large eggs (beaten with fork)
2   sticks salted butter (melted)
1   cup chopped onion
2   (10-ounce) packages frozen chopped broccoli florets (partially cooked and drained)
1   (8-ounce) container cottage cheese

1. Preheat oven to 425°. Grease a 13x9-inch casserole dish.
2. In a medium bowl, combine cornbread mix, eggs, melted butter, onion, broccoli, and cottage cheese. Mix well. Let stand for 5 minutes. Pour into prepared casserole dish.
3. Bake until golden brown, 30 to 40 minutes.

William is ready for vacation (above). Banks and I are all dressed up to go out.

"Your children, family, and friends sometimes just need to talk about what's on their minds. So, be quiet and listen."

HONEY BUTTER

—◆—

This sweetened butter makes all breads transform from ordinary to extraordinary. The secret is in the whipping. Whip! Whip! Whip! Once the butter is light and fluffy, glory—it's wonderful! My granddaughter Cape is the one who said, "Big Mama, you need to make honey butter."
So, of course, I learned.

1   pound unsalted butter (room temperature)
⅓   cup honey
1   tablespoon powdered sugar
¼   teaspoon sea salt

1. In a stand mixer, whip, whip, whip the butter for a long time. It will begin to look white in color.

2. Add honey and mix until combined. Add powdered sugar and mix. Stir in sea salt.

Walt, Hannah, and Cape at Little Friends Preschool

Here, I am making fried apple pies. Put Honey Butter on a warm pie, and it will make your heart sing.

KITCHEN WISDOM

Only use sea salt in this recipe. It makes a huge difference. The flaky shape of the salt crystals holds up and gives it a nice little crunch.

SWEET POTATO BISCUITS

My granddaughter Bay is known as "the middle biscuit girl." She will fight to get the biscuit in the middle of the pan. I know you have all learned how to make my buttermilk biscuits. Now, you can experiment with them. Throw in a little of this and a little of that until you create a brand-new dish. You will go back for more with these Sweet Potato Biscuits. Smear a big dollop of honey butter on them.

2	medium sweet potatoes (peeled and cut into chunks)
3	tablespoons sugar
⅓	cup whole milk
2	cups White Lily self-rising flour
1	stick salted butter (cut into 8 pieces)

1. Preheat oven to 450°. Grease a cast-iron skillet.
2. In a large pot, add potatoes and cover with water. Bring to a boil and cook until fork tender. Drain and let cool. Use a fork to mash up the potatoes. Then, spoon out 1½ cups mashed potato and set aside. (Save the rest for another use.)
3. Put the 1½ cups mashed potato, sugar, and milk in a food processor or stand mixer and process until mixture is puréed. Set aside.
4. Mix flour and butter in a food processor or stand mixer and process until mixture starts to form a grainy flour. Add potato mixture and process until a smooth dough. Don't overwork.
5. Flour a surface and your hands. Pat out the ball of dough and then fold over in thirds and pat down again. Do this twice. Press the dough down to ¾-inch thickness. Cut into squares or use a round cutter. Place the biscuits in the prepared skillet.
6. Bake for about 15 minutes, or until golden brown.

Bay making biscuits on Christmas Eve night

ROASTED GARLIC SPREAD

A spread that is so simple to make and so tasty—my whole family is addicted to this stuff. You can add roasted garlic to lots of recipes, like butter to serve with rolls or put a little in your vegetables for a nice flavor. Just use your imagination!

1   head garlic (unpeeled)
1   tablespoon olive oil (plus more for drizzling)
1   (8-ounce) package cream cheese (softened)
½   stick salted butter
¼   teaspoon salt
2   green onions (chopped)
1   loaf French bread or Italian bread

1. Preheat oven to 350°.
2. Peel off the outer skin from the garlic, leaving the head intact. Place the garlic head on its side and trim off the top with a sharp knife, just enough to show the raw garlic. On a piece of foil, place the head of garlic standing up with the root side down. Gently pour 1 tablespoon olive oil over the raw garlic. Fold up the foil over the garlic and put it in a small cast-iron skillet.
3. Bake for 25 minutes. Open the foil to uncover the garlic head and bake until garlic is soft, 8 minutes more. Remove from oven and let cool.
4. Turn the garlic upside down and squeeze the roasted garlic out into a small bowl. (Remove any papery skin that may have fallen into the bowl.)
5. In a stand mixer, beat cream cheese and butter at high speed until fluffy. Add roasted garlic, salt, and green onion and mix. Store in refrigerator.
6. When ready to serve, cut the bread into slices and lay flat on a pan. Drizzle olive oil on each piece. Heat the bread in the oven on broil until lightly brown. Smear the garlic spread on one piece of the toasted bread. Take a bite—so good!

KITCHEN WISDOM

You can store the garlic spread in the refrigerator, but when you're ready to serve it, be sure you let it come to room temperature.

chapter 10

THE SWEET STUFF

THE GOOD LORD KNOWS
WHAT WE NEED

I'm sitting here in the den on my brown leather couch looking out the big plate glass window and thinking about the hot, humid weather. The leaves on my plants are drooping, their heads hanging down craving water. The ground is hard and crusty with cracks, needing fresh rainwater. I'm tired of the hot weather, sticky skin, and sidewalks of asphalt and concrete that radiate the heat. My breathing is actually labored when I'm outside in this heavy air.

I'm thankful that the good Lord knows what we need before we even ask. He says in Matthew 6:8 that we don't have to stand in front of people and pray with lots of words. We can just go to the Lord with what's on our heart, and He will hear our cry. We can just speak the name of Jesus. Isn't that an amazing blessing!

It seems we humans need variety in every aspect of our lives. God gave us the seasons for that reason. For instance:

WINTER has its beautiful white snowflakes, frosty morning windowpanes, naked trees against a gray sky, thick evergreen trees, icicles, and children with cold, red noses.
SPRING brings new hope to our lives with bursting buds on every tree, sunny skies, excited children, the scent of flowers floating in the air, barefoot toes, and the smell of freshly plowed dirt.
SUMMER gives us long days and starry nights, thin cool clothing, thunderstorms, and beach vacations.
FALL comes with tumbling red and gold leaves, prickly pine straw, cool brisk nights, schoolchildren, open windows, and the delicious harvest.

We humans are forever changing our minds about everything because we love variety—paint color for our homes, clothing styles, hairstyles, colors and cuts, vehicles, different foods at each meal. We like variety, and that's OK. God made us that way. Just open your eyes and see His glory all around you. Smell all the different scents He has provided. Reach out with your fingertips and feel all the textures. Listen to the many sounds from crying babies, thunderstorms, choirs, birds, and the wind blowing through the trees. Think about all the flavors He has provided: fried chicken, sweet honey, vanilla, salt, herbs, sour lemons, and fresh vegetables.

When I think of the Lord, I can't help but smile. Scripture says we are made in His image. I know that's true. Why? Because God likes variety, too.

ICE CREAM SUNDAE PIE

You better get out a bunch of spoons when you make this recipe because you're going to need them! Ice cream, chocolate sauce, and pecans on a bed of vanilla wafers make this a scrumptious dessert for any occasion.

1   (11-ounce) box vanilla wafers
1   gallon vanilla ice cream
Chocolate Sauce (recipe follows)
1   cup roasted pecans (chopped)

1. In an 11x7-inch casserole dish, layer vanilla wafers, ice cream, and Chocolate Sauce, and then repeat the layers again. Cover with plastic wrap and place in freezer until ready to serve. Top with pecans just before serving.

Chocolate Sauce

¼   teaspoon salt
1   cup semisweet chocolate chips
1   cup mini marshmallows
1   cup evaporated milk

1. In the top of a double boiler, combine salt, chocolate chips, marshmallows, and evaporated milk. Cook until sauce thickens and let cool before pouring on ice cream.

KITCHEN WISDOM

It will be easier to slice if you take it out of the freezer and let it sit at room temperatue for a few minutes before serving.

MEMAMA'S LEMON-PINEAPPLE CAKE

I can't do a cookbook without one of my mama's glorious cakes. The grandchildren all called her MeMama, and she could make you feel special. You will make everyone feel special if you make this luscious coconut-covered cake. Put it on a pretty cake stand and set it on the buffet and just watch it disappear.

Cake:
1   (15.25-ounce) box lemon supreme cake mix
1   (3.4-ounce) box lemon instant pudding mix
1   teaspoon salt
¾   cup vegetable oil
1¼ cups lemon-lime soda
4   large eggs

Icing:
4½ cups sugar
6   tablespoons White Lily all-purpose flour
9   large egg yolks
3   (20-ounce) cans crushed pineapple (drained very well)
3   cups sweetened flaked coconut

1. Preheat oven to 325°. Grease and flour 3 (9-inch) round cake pans.
2. For the cake: Mix all cake ingredients, adding the eggs one at a time. (Do not use directions on the cake or pudding mixes.) Divide batter into prepared pans.
3. Bake until a wooden pick inserted in center comes out clean, about 25 minutes. Let cool in pans.
4. For the icing: In a small pot, mix all icing ingredients, except coconut. Cook, stirring frequently, over low heat until thickened and bubbly, about 30 minutes. Remove from heat and add coconut. Let cool.
5. Spread icing between each cake layer as you stack them. Finish off icing the cake with remaining icing. Place in refrigerator overnight.

THEREFORE, TO HIM THAT KNOWETH TO DO GOOD, AND DOETH IT NOT, TO HIM IT IS SIN. —JAMES 4:17, KJV

CHOCOLATE SWIRL PIE

You can top off this pie with a dollop of real whipped cream to dress it up if you like. Toast the pecans in a pan with a little bit of butter.

2 (8-ounce) packages cream cheese (softened)
1 cup sugar
1 (8-ounce) container frozen whipped topping (thawed)
5 (1-ounce) squares semisweet chocolate (melted)
2 tablespoons salted butter
1 (9-inch) graham cracker piecrust
Toasted pecan pieces

1. In a stand mixer, beat cream cheese and sugar at medium speed until smooth. Add in whipped topping.
2. Mix melted chocolate with butter. Fold melted chocolate into cream cheese mixture and spoon into piecrust. Top with toasted pecans. Refrigerate for several hours before serving.

"Be gentle with old folks. They may not walk as fast as you, and their words may be a little slower, but their wisdom and love for others is genuine."

Life's Collections

As you probably already know, I like wood or anything made from wood—bowls, rolling pins, utensils, butter molds, and chopping boards. Wooden kitchen utensils feel good in my hand and look great in an old bowl sitting on my table. I just grab one and start using it. The best ones are homemade. My sweet followers have given me some, like the zebra and fancy wooden spoons.

THE "BIG" (ANY FLAVOR) CAKE

There is nothing like a tall layer cake to impress your company. This one uses whatever cake mix you might have on hand. It goes nicely with my Buttercream Icing on page 249 and fresh strawberries on top.

1   (15.25-ounce) box desired flavor cake mix (do not follow instructions on box)
1   cup White Lily self-rising flour
½   cup sugar
1   cup whole buttermilk
1   cup water
¾   cup vegetable or canola oil
1   teaspoon vanilla extract
4   large eggs

1. Preheat oven to 350°. Grease and flour 3 (9-inch) round cake pans. (You also can make 3 [8-inch] cake layers, a sheet cake, or 24 cupcakes. See Kitchen Wisdom below.)
2. In a mixing bowl, combine cake mix, flour, and sugar, stirring with a fork or whisk.
3. In a large bowl, combine buttermilk, 1 cup water, oil, vanilla, and eggs, breaking egg yolks with a fork. Add the buttermilk mixture to flour mixture, in thirds or halves, and mix until well combined. (Mix in less time for a more tender cake; mix for longer for a slightly firmer crumb.) Pour into prepared pans.
4. Bake for 25 to 30 minutes.

Anna pours homemade eggnog in MeMama's kitchen at Christmastime.

KITCHEN WISDOM

In 8-inch round cake pans, bake for 30 to 35 minutes; in a 13x9-inch cake pan, bake for 35 to 40 minutes; and for 24 cupcakes, bake for 18 to 20 minutes. Since every oven is different, it's hard to know the exact baking time. When a wooden pick inserted in the center comes out clean, the cake is ready.

SWEET POTATO COBBLER

Your grandmother might have made this old-fashioned cobbler. Cut your sweet potatoes crosswise in 1-inch-thick circles, then use your knife to peel them. After you cube the sweet potatoes, put them in a bowl of water so they won't turn dark.

5 to 6 large sweet potatoes
1½ sticks salted butter
7 cups water
1¾ cups sugar
Dumpling Dough (recipe follows)
2 tablespoons salted butter (melted)

1. Preheat oven to 350°.
2. Peel potatoes and cut into 1-inch cubes.
3. In a large boiler, combine potatoes, butter, and 7 cups water. Bring to a boil over medium heat and cook just until tender. (Be careful not to overcook the potatoes or they will fall apart.) When tender, gently take potatoes out of the water and set aside. Leave the water in the pot (good flavor there) and add 1½ cups sugar to sweet potato water. Stir well.
4. Divide the Dumpling Dough into 2 balls. Roll out 1 ball as thin as possible on a lightly floured surface. (If the dough is sticks to the surface, then reroll into a ball and add more flour until it is just right.) Cut dumplings into 3x2-inch strips.
5. Bring the potato water back to a rolling boil and drop the dumplings into the water. Return to a rolling boil, turn heat down to medium, and cook until dumplings are tender, about 15 minutes. While the dumplings are boiling, go ahead and roll the remaining ball of dough to fit the top of

a deep 13x9-inch casserole dish.
6. When dumplings have cooked, gently pour the dumpling mixture and the sweet potatoes into your ungreased 13x9-inch casserole dish. Gently stir to combine. (The mixture should be very juicy.) Add your rolled dough to cover the top of the casserole dish. Let the dough go over the sides of the dish. Brush the melted butter over the top crust. Sprinkle the remaining ¼ cup sugar on top of the buttered crust.
7. Bake until crust is a beautiful light brown, about 30 to 40 minutes.

Dumpling Dough

3 cups White Lily all-purpose flour (sifted)
1 cup whole buttermilk
½ cup shortening

1. Mix flour, buttermilk, and shortening in a bowl. Knead together well. Keep adding flour, a little bit at a time, until the dough is no longer sticky.
2. On a floured surface, take the dough out of the bowl. Knead on the surface until you have a firm ball of dough. This is when you will decide if you need to sprinkle more flour on the dough.

BASIC WHITE CAKE

There's no doubt this will become your go-to recipe for a white cake. You can also bake this in two round pans or make cupcakes—whatever you need. Be sure to let it cool in the pan completely before removing the cake and icing it. Try it with my Spiced Cream Cheese Icing recipe below.

2   sticks unsalted butter, softened
2   cups sugar
2   large eggs (room temperature)
2   large egg whites (room temperature)
3   cups White Lily all-purpose flour
1   tablespoon baking powder
½   teaspoon salt
1   cup whole milk (room temperature)
2   teaspoons vanilla extract
¼   teaspoon almond extract

1. Preheat oven to 350°. Grease and flour a 13x9-inch cake pan.
2. In a stand mixer, beat butter and sugar at medium speed until fluffy, about 3 to 4 minutes. Add eggs and egg whites, one at a time, beating well.
3. In a bowl, stir together flour, baking powder, and salt. Gradually add flour mixture to butter mixture alternating with milk and beating after each addition. Stir in extracts. Pour batter into prepared pan.
4. Bake until a wooden pick inserted in center comes out clean, 35 to 40 minutes. Let cool in pans for 10 minutes. Remove from pans. See Kitchen Wisdom on page 239.

SPICED CREAM CHEESE ICING

Simple flavors shine in this icing. There's no need to add vanilla extract, as it will overpower the flavor. Use this icing on white cake, yellow cake, or my Sweet Potato Cake on page 181.

2   (8-ounce) packages cream cheese (softened)
1   stick salted butter (room temperature)
½   cup light brown sugar (firmly packed)
½   cup powdered sugar
1   teaspoon ground cinnamon

1. In a stand mixer, beat cream cheese and butter until light and fluffy.
2. Stir together brown sugar, powdered sugar, and cinnamon. Add sugar mixture to the cream cheese mixture. If the icing is too thick for your liking, simply stir in whole milk, a teaspoonful at a time, until you reach the desired consistency.

PUMPKIN PIE

Walt and William are the only ones in our family who have to have a pumpkin pie for Thanksgiving. To be honest, I've never liked pumpkin pie. But one Thanksgiving, they both asked me to make one. I decided to make up my own recipe for pumpkin pie, figuring I would have to eat it, too. I put things in the recipe that I liked, and of course, I had to put lots of homemade whipped cream on top. This recipe makes two pies, so it will serve a family gathering.

1   (8-ounce) package cream cheese (room temperature)
⅓   cup light brown sugar
1   (15-ounce) can pure pumpkin
1   (14-ounce) can sweetened condensed milk
4   large eggs
½   teaspoon ground cinnamon
½   teaspoon ground ginger
½   teaspoon ground cloves
½   teaspoon salt
2   tablespoons salted butter (melted)
2   (9-inch) deep-dish frozen piecrusts
Homemade whipped cream

1. Preheat oven to 350°.
2. In a stand mixer, beat cream cheese and brown sugar until smooth. Add pumpkin and mix well. Add sweetened condensed milk and mix well. Add eggs, one at a time, mixing well after each addition. Add cinnamon, ginger, cloves, and salt. Add melted butter. Divide filling between 2 piecrusts.
3. Bake until a slight jiggle in the middle, about 45 minutes. Serve with a dollop of homemade whipped cream for a really rich and special flavor.

Life's Little Moments

Giggling and laughing bring joyfulness. I can think of many times when William and Banks would jump out from behind a wall and scare me, nearly sending me to an early grave. Boy, what fun it was to get them back! What fun it is to do the unexpected!

BUTTERCREAM ICING

Sweet, lush buttercream is so perfect on so many cakes. You can mix things into the icing to give it a different look and flavor that will complement your cake. Go ahead, try some of your own ideas for add-ins.

1½ sticks salted butter (room temperature)
¼ cup solid vegetable shortening
1 teaspoon vanilla extract
1 (16-ounce) package powdered sugar
1 to 3 tablespoons heavy whipping cream

1. In a stand mixer, beat butter, shortening, and vanilla together until creamy. Slowly add powdered sugar to butter mixture, beating at medium speed until well combined, about 2 minutes. Scrape down the side of the bowl a few times while mixing.

2. Add cream, a tablespoonful at a time, until you reach desired consistency. Use firmer icing for filling and thinner icing for frosting and piping.

VARIATIONS:

Cookies and Cream: Add ½ cup crushed cream-filled chocolate sandwich cookies and 2 tablespoons milk and stir well.

Hot Chocolate: Add 3 to 4 pouches hot chocolate mix (without marshmallows) and 1 tablespoon milk and stir well.

Peppermint: Add 1 to 2 teaspoons peppermint emulsion and stir well. Top cake with crushed peppermint candy.

Strawberry: Add ½ cup finely chopped or smashed fresh strawberries and stir well.

"Your tongue can get you in lots of trouble, so keep it tucked inside closed lips."

KITCHEN WISDOM

You can add any emulsion flavoring or extract. Emulsions have a stronger, long-lasting flavor unlike extracts, which are diluted with alcohol.

BASIC YELLOW CAKE

———◆———

Sometimes, you just want a plain, old-fashioned yellow cake. With this recipe, you can make all different sizes—a sheet cake, a layer cake, or even cupcakes. As it turns out, it's not so plain after all when you can add just about any icing or topping on this cake. Try my Cookies and Cream Buttercream Icing on page 249.

3 cups White Lily all-purpose flour (sifted)
3 teaspoons baking powder
1 teaspoon kosher salt
1 cup unsalted butter, softened
2 cups sugar
4 large eggs, room temperature
1 cup whole milk
2 teaspoons vanilla extract

1. Preheat oven to 350°. Grease and flour 2 (9-inch) cake pans.
2. In a medium bowl combine flour, baking powder, and salt.

3. In a stand mixer, beat butter and sugar until creamy, about 2 to 3 minutes. Add eggs one at a time.
4. Gradually add flour mixture to butter mixture alternating with milk and beating after each addition. Beat in vanilla.
5. Divide batter between prepared pans. Bake until wooden pick inserted in center comes out clean, about 25 to 30 minutes. Cool in pan 10 minutes. See Kitchen Wisdom on page 239.

LABOUR NOT TO BE RICH; CEASE FROM THINE OWN WISDOM. WILT THOU SET THINE EYES UPON THAT WHICH IS NOT? FOR RICHES CERTAINLY MAKE THEMSELVES WINGS; THEY FLY AWAY AS AN EAGLE TOWARD HEAVEN.
—PROVERBS 23:4–5, KJV

LIVE LIFE'S MOMENTS, Y'ALL!

When things are quiet and still in my home, I catch myself reminiscing about precious memories of special people in my life. A song playing on the radio, a familiar smell coming from the kitchen, or a warm blanket on a cold winter night can trigger these sweet memories. Of course, my George is at the center of many memories. God didn't create us to live alone. Just as He made Eve for Adam, God created George for me and me for George. We loved, laughed, worked, played, and helped each other every single day. We lived life together, side by side. After several years of marriage, the Lord blessed us with two beautiful babies, Dallas and Hannah. The Lord knew we needed our children to rock, bathe, kiss their sweet heads and tiny toes, bandage their skinned knees, and dry their tears. Most of all, we needed to teach them about Jesus by word and by good example. Time passed, and my George went to Heaven. I was left here alone because God had a plan for me, just the same as He has plans for you. We can't see the future, but when we look back, our lives fit together like a thousand pieces of a puzzle. Each piece has a perfect place to go, and the puzzle is finished when our life on earth is done. The whole puzzle picture will be beautifully completed. So, my friends, live life's moments to the fullest. Don't skip a single part. Hug when you can, dance in the kitchen, be ever so close to your mate, rock and kiss your children, spoil those grandbabies with chocolate chip cookies, and love the Lord your God with all your heart, soul, and mind. Don't fret about your to-do list for tomorrow. Remember, Matthew 6:34 asks us to not worry about tomorrow but to live in the present. Live your life, y'all. Live it to the fullest.

EDITOR'S NOTE Sitting on Brenda Gantt's front porch swing while enjoying her freshly made Sweet Potato Cobbler, you understand exactly what she means about appreciating the little moments in life. She tells us how her mother and grandmother made cobbler like this. Before long, conversation turns to a wooden pig decoration nearby filled with multicolored rocks, each with its own story. We learn Brenda's late husband, George, also had an Native American rock collection. Although he is no longer with us, George's presence is strong among the members of this loving, close-knit family. We enjoy a second helping of cobbler. Life slows down for a moment as we bask in the warmth of spring and admire the beauty of blooms all around. We watch chirping birds build nests in Brenda's scattered wooden birdhouses—another collection! Before long, it's back to work, and you realize this is a woman who truly practices what she preaches—live each little moment, y'all. —Marie Baxley

RECIPE INDEX

RESOURCES

Follow Brenda Gantt on Facebook at *facebook.com/cookingwithbrendagantt*.

To find writings by Walt Merrell, follow Shepherding Outdoors on Facebook at *facebook.com/shepherdingoutdoors*.

For more information about The Cottle House Bed & Breakfast, visit *thecottlehouse.com*.

To find White Lily products, visit *whitelily.com*.

For more information on Andalusia, Alabama, visit *cityofandalusia.com*.

All personal photography was provided by Brenda Gantt.

EDITORIAL

Founder
Phyllis Hoffman DePiano

President/Chief Creative Officer
Brian Hart Hoffman

EVP/Chief Content Officer
Brooke Michael Bell

Editorial Director
Marie Baxley

Art Director
Karissa Brown

Senior Editor
Kristi Fleetwood

Contributing Editor
Anna Hartzog

Copy Editor
Adrienne Davis

Test Kitchen Director
Laura Crandall

Food Stylists
Katie Moon Dickerson, Kathleen Kanen, and Vanessa Rocchio

Senior Prop Stylist
Sidney Bragiel

Prop Stylists
Maghan Armstrong, Courtni Bodiford, Maggie Hill, and Donna Nichols

Photographers
Jim Bathie, Kyle Carpenter, and John O'Hagan

Senior Digital Imaging Specialist
Delisa McDaniel

PRODUCTION & MARKETING

President/Chief Executive Officer
Eric Hoffman

EVP/Chief Operating Officer
Greg Baugh

EVP/Chief Marketing Officer
Missy Polhemus

VP/Marketing
Kristy Harrison

Associate Marketing Manager
Morgan Barbay

COVER
Photography by Jim Bathie, and styling by Sidney Bragiel and Vanessa Rocchio

A SPECIAL THANK YOU

It's hard for me to even comprehend that my third cookbook is completed. Not an easy task for sure. The good Lord provided a way, so I walked through the door. Friends and family came together as a unit with one goal in mind: a third cookbook. The Hoffman team did just that. Marie, Vanessa, Sydney, and Jim have spent many hours at the office and right here in my kitchen with me. I cooked; they took pictures and notes; we laughed and then I cooked some more. Together, we made it happen so that all my family and followers could enjoy the fruits of our labor. Thank you, Hannah, for helping me organize and proofread the book. A huge thanks to Shonna Reeves, who is so efficient in keeping all my recipes typed and organized, and Gloria Day, who helped with all my daily chores giving me time to work on my book. Thanks to Anna and Hannah for helping gather up our family's favorite recipes. I always enjoy reading the Forewords: book one by my daughter, Hannah; book two by my son, Dallas; and book three by my son-in-law, Walt. They have all been a part of this, and the words that each of them wrote are so very special to me. To my followers: a special thanks!! You hung right here with me with encouragement all along the way. The followers made it possible. Without them, there would be no book.

—Brenda

Dear Lord,

I'm not worthy to even speak your holy name. And yet, when George came to be with you, you created a purpose for me. It was nurtured and born within my heart—a longing to leave our children and grandchildren with a book that would have recipes, family stories, and your holy word sprinkled all through the pages. You work in ways we don't understand, but we are made whole and with purpose when we cleave to you, Lord.

I don't know who holds this cookbook in their hands at this very moment, but I know your amazing love for them will never end. While glancing through these pages, I pray that we all realize how much we need you. Draw us closer to you, Lord, every hour of every day.

This old world is full of lost and dying people, searching for peace, hope, and happiness that can't be found in food, stuff, trips, material things, people, friends, or even family. They are not at peace within themselves; they are without hope and without real joy. Lord, reveal yourself to their hearts as they glance through the pages of this book.

Thank you, Lord, for loving me and giving your life.

Your child,
Brenda